IS
YOUR
HOUSE
HAUNTED?

About the Author

Debi Chestnut has been able to see and speak to ghosts her whole life. A paranormal researcher for twenty-five years, she gives lectures and conducts workshops in order to help people understand paranormal activity. She lives in southeastern Michigan.

Please visit her website, www.debichestnut.com, or her Facebook fan page, Debi Chestnut's Paranormal Realm. You can also contact her by e-mail, at debichestnut@yahoo .com.

IS
YOUR
HOUSE
HAUNTED?

Poltergeists, Ghosts or Bad Wiring

Debi Chestnut

Llewellyn Publications
Woodbury, Minnesota

First Edition
First Printing, 2011

Cover images: House: iStockphoto.com/Christine Glade, Girl: iStockphoto.com/
    Debi Bishop
Cover design by Lisa Novak

Llewellyn Publications is a registered trademark of Llewellyn Worldwide Ltd.

Library of Congress Cataloging-in-Publication Data

Chestnut, Debi.
  Is your house haunted? : poltergeists, ghosts, or bad wiring / Debi Chestnut. — 1st
ed.
      p.   cm.
  Includes bibliographical references.
  ISBN 978-0-7387-2681-6
  1. Haunted houses 2. Ghosts. 3. Parapsychology. I. Title. II. Title: Poltergeists,
ghosts, or bad wiring.
  BF1475.C44 2011
  133.1—dc22
                                        2011009248

Llewellyn Worldwide Ltd. does not participate in, endorse, or have any authority
or responsibility concerning private business transactions between our authors and
the public.
    All mail addressed to the author is forwarded, but the publisher cannot, unless spe-
cifically instructed by the author, give out an address or phone number.
    Any Internet references contained in this work are current at publication time,
but the publisher cannot guarantee that a specific location will continue to be main-
tained. Please refer to the publisher's website for links to authors' websites and
other sources.

Llewellyn Publications
A Division of Llewellyn Worldwide Ltd.
2143 Wooddale Drive
Woodbury, MN 55125-2989
www.llewellyn.com

Printed in the United States of America

Other books by Debi Chestnut

So You Want to Be a Ghost Hunter?

Ghosts of Anchor Bay (with Linda Sparkman)

Legacy of the Cross (with Alice Bliss)

Murder in Crystal: A Savannah Williams Mystery

Telltale Signs: A Savannah Williams Mystery

I dedicate this book to my husband, Lonnie, for his patience; to James and the rest of the team at Black River Paranormal for their assistance and friendship; to all of the spirits I've met on my journey; and, most of all, to my readers, who make it all worthwhile.

Happy hauntings!

Contents

Introduction

Because I grew up in a house occupied by spirits, I understand how terrifying such an experience can be. However, most spirits are friendly and don't mean to scare us. It's just that we've been conditioned since childhood to be afraid of ghosts, and in some cases that fear is justified. Yet when it comes to spirits, fear is your real enemy. Some spirits feed off the fear and become stronger. Your best defense is to show no fear and deal with spirits in a logical, calm, and assertive manner.

How do I know this? I'm a "sensitive." To put it bluntly, I was born with the ability to see and talk to dead people. I've also been a paranormal researcher for the past twenty-five years.

One of my earliest memories as a child is of a ghost named Nathaniel, who lived on the second story, which was only used for storage, of my great-aunt's home in southeastern Michigan. Nathaniel and I spent countless hours up there playing amongst the books, furniture, and other miscellaneous items that, as a child, I found fascinating. Nathaniel was my first best friend.

Other spirits who visited me in the dark of night, however, were not so friendly, and I can remember being terrorized by them. They would wake me up and loom by my bed, asking for help. At that age, I had no idea how to help them.

My parents were fond of museums, antique stores, and other places filled with history, and we would often visit these places on the weekends. For me, these trips were torturous. Spirits would come forward and surround me. They always wanted something, and I still don't know what that "something" was. They would touch my hair, my shoulders, and be right up in my face yelling at me to help them. This would scare me, and it soon led me to being punished, because I became almost hysterical wanting to get out of there. You see, back when I was a child, most people didn't know how to deal with a "gifted" or psychic child, and we were often labeled mentally ill.

From the time I was four or five years old, my parents, who had adopted me when I was a baby, took me from psychiatrist to psychiatrist trying to find out what was "wrong" with me. Finally, when none of them had answers, and my parents refused to institutionalize me, my "gifts" were chalked up to an overactive imagination. A psychiatrist told my parents as much, but I know he knew the truth. My parents were "comfortable" with his answer and were relieved that I wasn't mentally disturbed, so they accepted his label for me: I was a creative child with an overactive imagination. It worked for them.

I think I was one of the lucky ones, because I can't imagine how many children in the 1950s and 1960s were institutionalized because they were gifted. I learned quickly how to hide my gifts, and I spent a lot of my childhood living in quiet terror of the ghostly specters who frequently visited my room.

As I got older, I learned how to help them and how to communicate with them, but this was not by choice—it was by necessity. I also learned how to control my gift and only let in the spirits I wanted, when I wanted. I wish I could share with you how I did that, but honestly I don't know. It's different for everyone who can do what I do, who sees what I see. We all come up with defense mechanisms and ways not only to protect ourselves but also to cope with everyday life. For me, everyday life includes dealing with the ghosts and spirits of people who have passed on.

As an adult, I honed my abilities so that I could help people who are experiencing paranormal events and don't know or understand how to deal with them. This led me to the field of paranormal research.

It's been my experience that ghosts and spirits mostly want to be acknowledged in some way. Sometimes they have a message they want to convey, and other times I think they are as curious about me as I am about them.

Almost all of the e-mails and telephone conversations I have with people who may be experiencing the paranormal start out with one of two sentences: "You're going to think I'm crazy" or "This may sound weird, but . . . " The truth is you're not going crazy, and weird is pretty much my normal.

Thousands of people, if not hundreds of thousands of people, are living in fear of possible ghosts or spirits in their homes. A 2007 poll by the Associated Press revealed that one in three Americans believe in ghosts. Another poll by Pew Research showed that almost one in five Americans believe they have been in the presence of a ghost or have seen a ghost. These are quite startling statistics, given that there are more than 300 million people in the United States. Yet what many people don't realize is that help is available. No reason exists for you to live in fear in your own home.

My years as a paranormal researcher have taught me that some people who are living with apparent ghosts or spirits are often either afraid or embarrassed to tell anyone about what they're experiencing. These people might be worried that whoever they tell will laugh at them, not believe them, or think less of them. The truth of the matter is that no one should have to suffer in silence. Don't be afraid to tell someone what you're experiencing.

The purpose of this book is to provide help for those of you who are being haunted, or believe you are being haunted. In many cases there is a logical explanation for what you're experiencing, and my goal is to help you to determine if your home is being shared by spirits and, if so, how to cope with them.

This book will give you the tools necessary to empower yourself and your family so that no one in your home has to live in fear. You will learn about different types of ghosts and spirits, as well as the different types of hauntings. No two hauntings are alike, but each type of haunting has its own characteristics.

Knowing not only what type of ghost or spirit you're dealing with, but also the type of haunting you may be experiencing, will help alleviate your fear. Just as with most things in life, once you know what you're dealing with, the anxiety in most cases will evaporate, and you will be able to come up with a plan to handle the ghosts in your home.

You should also know that you're not alone. I'm right there with you every step of the way.

CHAPTER 1

Your House Could
Be Haunted If...

*S*trange things are happening in your home, unusual events that can't always be explained away. Out of the corner of your eye, you're seeing something or someone move. Your pets are behaving strangely. You begin to ask yourself . . . is my house haunted?

A true haunting is very rare, but when it happens the unsettling events can be frightening. Sometimes it's not easy to determine if your home is actually haunted, or if there is a logical explanation for the string of unexplained occurrences.

What follows in this chapter is a checklist of phenomena that could indicate your home is being shared with a ghost. No two hauntings are alike, as I've mentioned, although they share some common denominators.

There is a difference between an actual haunting and paranormal activity. In order to be considered haunted, the activity you are experiencing must be consistent and the spirit must be intelligent. By *intelligent*, I mean able to acknowledge the living in some manner. I will discuss this topic in more detail later in the book.

Some people may find the examples I use in this book scary, but stop and think about what is happening in your own home. Are you or any other family member being harmed? My guess is probably not. Instead, you're most likely just being startled, which makes you scared.

Hollywood has filled our minds with thoughts that we should be scared by or afraid of ghosts. The plain truth is that most of the time we are manifesting our own fear, because we've been conditioned since childhood into doing so.

If the ghost or spirit in your home is not harming you or anyone else in any manner, then stop and think, "Am I being harmed?" the next time a paranormal event occurs. By changing your inner dialogue, you will stop being so frightened every time something happens.

Those people who *are* being threatened or harmed by a negative or angry ghost should seek help as soon as possible. These types of spirits are unpredictable and can, in many cases, become violent or aggressive very quickly.

Now, let's roll up our sleeves and get to work. As you go through the following list, you may want to grab a pen and paper and take notes of the activity that you or any member of your household is currently experiencing or has experienced in the past.

The goal of this chapter is to help you identify the types of activities you're experiencing and attempt to find a logical explanation for those events.

Electrical Events

For some reason, ghosts or spirits appear to be able to manipulate electrical items with relative ease.

One theory is that ghosts are made up of energy. Simple science teaches us that energy reacts to energy. Thus, turning on or off a light could easily be accomplished by a spirit.

Lights are not the only electrical items ghosts can manipulate. There have been reports of ghosts turning on stereos, televisions, and other electrical appliances. Some ghosts have been known to make a television change channels at a rapid rate of speed, or even play with the volume on both TVs and radios.

While this type of activity can be unnerving to the living, no one is being harmed by these events, and in many cases it is simply the ghost wanting to be acknowledged in some way. If you suspect a ghost is causing this type of activity, in a calm voice tell the ghost that you know it is there and you would greatly appreciate it if it would stop playing with the lights, radio, television, or whatever electrical device the ghost is attracted to. In most cases, this is enough to make the activity stop for a short period of time.

It also tells you that the ghost is an intelligent being and capable of communicating with the living. This bit of information can work in your favor and is an important piece of information, as you will find out in later chapters.

Look for a logical explanation to the activity by checking all the cords and wiring to any electrical items that are either flickering or going on and/or off by themselves. Look for any torn outer casing on the cords or wires as well. Don't forget to check the seam in the center of the cord for rips or tears. Replace any cords that look suspicious. Also, if lights are flickering it could be that you have a bad light bulb or the bulb is ready to burn out. Change the light bulb and see if this stops the activity.

If you use any lights or ceiling fans with a transmitter in them for a remote control or wall switch, try changing the frequency. I've personally experienced this problem: our neighbors installed a ceiling fan with a remote control in their house. Every time they turned on or off the light, my ceiling fan in the dining room of my house turned on or off. After we changed the frequency on the transmitter, the problem stopped.

If any of the above doesn't solve the problem, hire a licensed electrician to check all the switches, outlets, and wiring in your home for possible problems that could be causing the type of activity you're experiencing. However, sometimes there is a paranormal explanation.

As another example, my father, who has passed away, was terribly fond of electrical gadgets and practical jokes. In my office is a ceiling fan that is equipped with a light. My husband, also fond of gadgets, installed a switch for the fan in place of a normal light switch. It is equipped with three fan speeds and the light control, including a dimmer.

There I am sitting in my office writing, and suddenly the light, which is always set to full brightness, will dim down almost to total darkness and then go back to full strength. It will then dim again, go bright, and then dim and stay there. I will then say, "Dad, weren't you the one who always said reading in the dark will ruin my eyes?" The light will then go back to full brightness and remain there for the rest of the night.

It's just my dad's way of saying that he's here, and while it may seem scary to some, it brings me comfort to know he's still being my dad and that we can still share a laugh or two.

As you can see, not all ghosts are bad. The spirit of loved ones who have passed away can bring the same comfort to the living as they did in life, just in a slightly different manner.

In some cases, having a ghost who can manipulate electrical items can be very handy. In one of our homes, we had a ghost that aimed to please. I came home after a day of shopping for Christmas presents. My husband was at work; he worked afternoons, and I'd forgotten to leave lights on before I left the house earlier that day.

Anyway, my arms were filled with shopping bags, and I was eight months pregnant. Needless to say, it was all I could do to get the key in the door to unlock it. Knowing that one of the ghosts in the house liked to turn lights on and off, I walked into the house and yelled, "Could someone get the lights, please?" Sure enough, the foyer light and the dining room light turned themselves on, giving me a clear, lighted path. After setting down my packages on the table, I thanked the ghost for its help and went about my business.

I know: weird. But like I said, weird is pretty much my normal.

Unexplained Noises

Most people know the common noises their own home makes, so it's not uncommon to notice when something sounds out of place. For example, you may hear footsteps or the sound of something being moved, dragged, or dropped.

Some ghosts will knock on doors or walls, while others may make rapping, thumping, or scratching noises. All of these noises can either be quite loud or very subdued.

If you're experiencing this type of activity, take note of the time of day, who was in the house, including any pets, where they were, and the day and date the event occurred. This could be important information later on.

Try to debunk the activity. Remember, houses naturally make noise. The furnace or air conditioner can come on or turn off; the sump pump, if you have one, runs, and so on. New homes settle, old homes creak and groan. Get to know the sounds your house makes so you will recognize when something sounds out of place.

If you hear what sounds like footsteps, it could be the wind, the floors settling, or a pipe or air duct rattling against a joist or rafter. Rule these and any other possible causes out before making the assumption that a ghost is walking down the hall or stairway.

Scratching noises in the walls could be animals. Birds, bats, raccoons, mice, or other small animals can get stuck in chimneys. Mice and other animals can get into your walls or attic. Hire a reputable critter-control service to check your home for animals if you're experiencing this type of activity.

Check for tree limbs or branches rubbing against the outside walls or roof of your home for a possible explanation as well.

Rapping, tapping, and/or banging can be explained by loose siding, shutters, or wood on the outside of your home. This type of activity can also be explained by a loose water pipe banging against a beam or joist. Inspect your home from top to bottom, inside and out, in an attempt to explain logically the noises you are hearing.

Sometimes it's something as simple as the floor vibrating slightly as the furnace turns on, or air rushing through the ductwork in your home.

An example: I got an e-mail early one evening from an obviously terrified woman who was experiencing strange noises coming from the family room in her house. This activity had been occurring over a period of a week or so.

I contacted the family and went over to their house the next day. The first thing I noticed was the enormous fireplace and chimney on the back wall of the room.

After confirming with the family that that area of the room seemed to be having the most activity, I scampered up to the second floor, crawled out their bathroom window onto the roof of the family room, and, with a strong flashlight in hand, peered down the chimney. Sure enough, as it was early spring, a family of raccoons had taken up residence in the chimney.

We called a critter-control company and mama raccoon and her babies were safely extracted from their nesting place and carefully relocated to a more appropriate spot. Case closed. You may be asking yourself, "How did she even think of that?" The truth is I had a family of raccoons take up residence in my fireplace one spring, so to me it was the most obvious place to start.

Doors Opening and Closing

Many different types of ghosts enjoy opening and closing doors, cabinets, and kitchen cupboards. This type of activity can be very confusing and frustrating for the living. You may swear the doors were closed when you left the room, only to return a few minutes later and find one or all of them open. To answer your question: if you're rational enough to ask if you're going crazy, you're not going crazy.

In some cases, you may hear doors opening or being slammed shut. Doors that are locked could be unlocked and vice versa. The doors, cabinets, or cupboards might open or close very slowly or with a violent force behind them.

Many people chalk up this type of activity to being forgetful, thinking they really weren't paying attention to what they were doing and can't remember whether or not they shut or opened a door. However, if doors, cabinets, and/or cupboards are opening or closing in front of your eyes, it's a little hard to dismiss.

Try to duplicate this type of activity. Sometimes a door is off center or hung improperly. This can cause the door to open or close by itself. Also check the door's closing mechanism. Make sure that when the door is closed, a breeze, someone walking by it, or a gentle nudge or bump can't open it.

If a door slams shut, try pushing it gently to see if you can duplicate the slamming. Check the hinges for proper functioning as well. The same thing applies to kitchen cabinets and other doors: sometimes a simple adjustment or tightening of the hinges can solve the problem.

Sometimes a vacuum is created between an interior door and an exterior door, which can cause the door to either open or slam shut by itself. I've personally had this happen many times.

Furniture or Other Objects Being Moved

While it's extremely rare, it is possible for furniture or other objects to be moved from one place to another. Even rarer is for someone to witness this type of event.

As an example, you may walk through your dining room and notice all the chairs pushed in to the table. A little while later you go back into the dining room and one or more chairs are now moved away from the table.

The same applies to knickknacks or other objects. They could be in one place when you leave the room, and in an entirely different place or missing altogether when you return to the room a little while later.

Make sure other members of your household didn't move the furniture or rearrange the knickknacks. Furniture can be moved by a pet or someone accidently bumping into it, and chances are the person won't even remember doing it.

If you have a cleaning crew, the explanation could be there. It's not uncommon for things to be left out of place in that circumstance.

Obviously, if your kitchen chairs are being stacked on your table, or large pieces of furniture are moved across the room with no plausible explanation, you have an issue and should seek the help of a qualified paranormal investigator immediately.

In our first home, my husband hung shelves by the window of our son's bedroom. These shelves were secured into the wall with molly bolts. I'd told him not to hang them there because the ghost that lived upstairs liked to look out that window. Of course my husband didn't listen.

The next weekend we went out of town. Upon returning, we found the shelves ripped out of the wall—leaving gaping holes from the molly bolts in the wall. Needless to say, the shelves were re-hung in a different part of the room, and were left alone by the spirit.

This example shows that it is possible to cohabitate with a ghost if you're willing to compromise.

As another example, when we moved into our current house I knew there was a shadow person here. I'd seen him on the stairs several times. More about shadow people will be explained later in this chapter. Anyway, I kept finding the drawers in our upstairs bathroom vanity open. Not all the time, mind you, just once in a while.

My first instinct was to blame it on the shadow person. However, one day I went upstairs to clean the bathroom and noticed the bottom drawer was open. I went to shut it, but it wouldn't close. Upon further investigation, I discovered one of my cats sleeping behind the open drawer! I didn't even know my cats could open drawers. Mystery solved.

So, as you see, there is generally a logical explanation to seemingly paranormal events!

Missing Objects

Let's assume you put something in the same spot every time you use it—your car keys, for example. You reach to grab them and they're gone. You race through the house searching for them: you dig through your purse, coat pockets, pants, couch cushions, and you still can't find them. Just when you've given up, you find them right where they should have been.

In some cases, items may be gone for days, weeks, months, or even years before they resurface, normally in plain sight.

I've noticed over the years that some ghosts are fond of shiny objects such as keys, coins, jewelry, and so on. This does not mean the ghost won't hide other items as well.

Let's face it: we're all absent-minded at one time or another, and this is normally the cause of such activity, especially when it comes to keys. But if this is happening on a consistent basis, you may want to take note of it.

If an item of jewelry goes missing, check to see if someone in your family borrowed it. Also try to remember the last time you wore it, and where you put it when you took it off. It could just be misplaced. If not, pay attention to the piece of jewelry missing, especially if it belonged to a relative who has passed, or if it is a family heirloom. This could be your loved one's way of saying he or she is still around you and wants you to know that. Don't worry, your loved one will replace the missing piece of jewelry . . . eventually.

On a personal note, I have a broach that belonged to my aunt. I always kept it in my jewelry box on the top shelf of my bedroom closet. Two weeks after I discovered it missing, I was walking through the living room and it literally fell out of nowhere and landed at my feet.

You see, this is how many spirits communicate with us, especially spirits of the loved ones who have passed away. It is just their little way of telling us they are around.

As another example, I always put my keys in the same spot every time I walk into the house. Once in a while, though, I will reach for my keys and they won't be where I put them. So I do the obvious mad search through the house. Finally, I will just say, "I'm leaving the room for five minutes. When I come back in here, my keys better be where they were." Five minutes later I'll walk back into the room, and sure enough, my keys are right where I left them. I thank the spirit for returning my keys and out the door I go.

I personally find this type of mischievous behavior amusing, but then again I have kind of a strange sense of humor. Most of the time it is just the ghost trying to get your attention, or wanting you to acknowledge it in some way, so there's no cause for alarm.

This can work in reverse as well. By that I mean that there have been cases when a spirit drops coins or other things at someone's feet without that person ever owning the object or realizing the item was missing.

There's no reason to be scared by such events. Normally it is a loved one letting you know he or she is there, and it is the only way the spirit has found to communicate with you.

Unexplained Smells and Odors

The scent of perfume, flowers, pipe tobacco, cigar or cigarette smoke, or other odors may appear to fill a room. The smells seem to come and go for no apparent reason, and are often in conjunction with some other event. The smells may linger or disappear as quickly as they appear.

When you notice a particular smell or odor, try to determine the cause immediately. Check for open doors, windows, or children playing with something they shouldn't be.

Take care to notice if the smell is coming from just one room, throughout several rooms, or encasing the entire house.

Try to determine what the smell is. For example, if your washer is filling or draining, you could be smelling the laundry detergent. If the dryer is on and you use fabric softener sheets, that could be the cause of the aroma.

If the odor is foul, check for backed-up sewer drains, septic tank problems, or mold and mildew. If you suspect mold or mildew, make sure you check your closets, the cabinets in your kitchen and bathroom, and every inch of your basement and attic.

Take particular notice if a smell is more noticeable when the furnace or air conditioning is on. Odors can travel through the ductwork in your home and be circulated through one or more rooms.

My great-aunt always wore Chantilly perfume. Unfortunately, I am allergic to it and would sneeze every time I caught a whiff of it. Upon my great-aunt's passing, my husband and I moved into her home.

When she was alive, my great-aunt would always sit at the dining room table working on her crossword puzzles. It became my habit to sit in the same spot she used to sit in. Every once in a while, while sitting at the table, I would be surrounded by the smell of Chantilly perfume, causing me to sneeze violently a few times. Then the scent would disappear as quickly as it came.

The whole time I lived in her house, I would also smell her perfume at various times around the baby's crib and in other parts of the house. To me it was nice to know she was still maintaining our close relationship even though she was no longer living.

Many times the spirits of our loved ones do come back to let us know they are there and watching over us, or that they are okay. When they do this, it's nothing to be afraid of, and it doesn't mean your house is haunted. It just means that someone you loved very much is still close to you. My experience has been that once you've been able to identify the ghost or spirit that is sharing your home, in most cases the fear goes away because you know what you're dealing with.

As another example, a friend of mine would "pick up" a passenger almost every time she was coming from my house and leaving my house. The route she took to my home led her past a cemetery. As soon as she got to the cemetery, she'd notice the strong smell of cherry pipe tobacco coming from the back seat of her truck. When she passed a certain old home on the street, about a half mile away from the cemetery, the smell would disappear when she stopped at the stop sign by that house.

The same thing would happen in reverse when she left my house. She'd smell the pipe tobacco when she stopped at the intersection by that house, and the smell would disappear as soon as she passed the cemetery.

This was not constant activity, mind you, just every once in a while. We never did figure out who it was, but she didn't mind giving her ghostly passenger a ride, although I do remember her saying on several occasions that she never really dared to look in the rear-view mirror to see if anything was in the back seat of her car.

Audible Voices

In your home you may hear whispering, crying, or screaming. Some people have even reported hearing their name being called or other words spoken when they were alone in their homes.

Cases exist in which people report hearing music playing that sounds as though it is coming from a radio or musical instrument. While much of this type of activity can be a sign of a residual haunting, which will be explained in more detail in chapter 3, there are some occasions when it is not—for example, if you have a piano and you hear it playing in the middle of the night.

This type of activity can easily be explained away as simply our mind playing tricks on us. Another possibility is a clock radio or television being left on or noise from a neighbor's home.

Listen carefully to determine whether the sound came from inside or outside your home. If inside, try to figure out which room the voice or music came from and investigate that room from top to bottom for any possible cause.

In our current house, this type of activity occurred just recently. I was home by myself and in the laundry room folding clothes. The television and radios were all off. I distinctly heard a woman's voice call out from the living room, "Hello, hello." Thinking it to be one of my neighbors, I went to the door and saw no one. I checked all the doors and outside, but there was not a living soul in sight.

Does this one event mean my house is haunted? Not by a long shot. It was a one-time occurrence and, while I still can't explain it, there is no reason for me to be concerned or scared.

Cold or Hot Spots

One of the most frequently reported symptoms associated with a haunting is experiencing cold spots or hot spots in one or more rooms of your home. The rest of the room might be at normal temperature, but one spot will be colder or hotter. The cold or hot spot may slowly travel across the room or appear to jump across the room.

It's also possible to experience one room always being colder or hotter than any other rooms in the house. Keep an eye out for sudden drops or rapid rises in temperature in rooms.

Some paranormal researchers believe that a cold spot indicates that a spirit is either just entering or leaving a room, or is trying to manifest itself in the room.

The theory behind this is that ghosts need a lot of energy to show themselves or manipulate objects in their environment. In order to do this, they suck the energy out of a room like a vacuum, thereby causing a sudden drop in temperature in that particular room.

Weather can play a huge part in creating cold spots. Check the direction the wind is coming from, especially in the winter. A strong, cold wind hitting the outside wall of a room can cause a cold spot.

In some cases, because the furnace is so far away from the room that is cold, the ductwork leading from the furnace has to run across the entire length of your house and/or up a flight of stairs. Less heat is therefore getting to that room. Check to make sure the heat vents are open in the room where you experience cold spots.

If you're unsure, hire a furnace company to inspect your furnace and ductwork. If necessary, have all the ductwork in your home cleaned by a reputable company. Also ensure there is proper insulation in your walls and attic.

Check the weather stripping around windows and doors. Even the tiniest of air leaks can cause cold or hot spots. Make sure all the seals are in good condition and free from rips and tears. Replace any worn-out seals and apply a fresh bead of caulk around any windows or doors as necessary.

On one of my paranormal investigations, my team and I ran into a cold spot in one of the bedrooms. We spent well over an hour trying to debunk it, but to no avail. The cold spot kept moving on us and would send our electromagnetic meters crazy, one of the signs that a spirit may be present. We chased that cold spot around that house the better part of two hours. I'm sure the ghost was greatly amused and having great fun. The team and I . . . yeah, not so much.

Feeling of Being Watched

The feeling of being watched is not uncommon and could be attributed to many different things. Nevertheless, if this feeling occurs in certain spots in your home and is consistent, there's a possibility it could be a paranormal event.

The feeling of someone following you down a hallway or flight of stairs would fall into this category as well. In a small town near where I live, the local historical society is housed in what used to be an old hotel. Many people, including me, have felt someone follow them down the stairs in that building on more than one occasion.

A mother brought her young son to one of my book signings, and they'd just been to a function at the historical society. The young lad was obviously shaken up, and his mom told me he'd felt someone follow him down the staircase in the building. I spent a few minutes talking to this young man and explained to him that I'd felt it too, but the ghost in that building wasn't there to hurt him; it was just curious about who he was and what he was doing there. A look of total relief washed over the boy's face when he realized he was not alone and someone believed him. He learned then what the spirit wanted and that it was harmless.

The old adage holds true: knowledge is power.

Keep in mind, though, that the human mind and senses can easily be deceived. Most of the time, this type of activity can be dismissed as imagination. Take note of what you or others are feeling and thinking right before you or they got the feeling. See if there's a connection and if it's possible that it's just your mind playing tricks on you or others.

It's possible for one or more rooms in your home to contain what some paranormal researchers call a *fear cage*. A fear cage is created when there is a high electromagnetic field present.

An electromagnetic field is generally caused by electrical wires or the circuit or fuse box. Cell phones and microwave ovens even emit some amount of electromagnetic field.

The theory is that electromagnetic energy has a direct effect on our brains and could cause such things as hallucinations, the feeling of being watched, paranoia, and so on.

Do a visual inspection of your home inside and out. Locate the fuse or circuit box and check for high-tension wires outside your home. Try to determine if the feelings you are experiencing could be caused by elevated levels of electromagnetic energy.

You can purchase an electromagnetic detector relatively cheaply if you want to totally eliminate a fear cage as the culprit. As an alternative, a good electrician should be able to determine if the electromagnetic levels in one or more rooms of your house are higher than normal.

Animals Behaving Strangely

Your dog may bark, growl, or wag its tail at something you can't see. The dog may be refusing to go into a room it would normally enter.

If you have a cat, it may seem to be following something across a room. It might, for some inexplicable reason, take a defensive posture such as hissing, or stand all its fur on end to appear larger.

Cats, dogs, and other animals might suddenly run from a room and act scared or refuse to enter that room again.

In other cases, your dog may stare at apparently nothing but be wagging its tail or playing with something or someone unseen. While unnerving to say the least, if there is a ghost present and playing with your dog or cat, at least you know the ghost is not there to cause any harm.

Many researchers believe that because animals have heightened senses, they could have more psychic abilities than humans or be able to see and sense things that we, as human beings, cannot. If there was something negative or dangerous there, your pet would not be playing with it. Your pet would either take a defensive stance or flee from the room.

Many pets, including dogs and cats, have extraordinary senses. Their eyesight, hearing, and sense of smell are many times that of humans. If your dog or cat is acting strangely, maybe your pet is seeing, smelling, and/or hearing something we can't. It could be a noise outside or a tiny bug crawling up a wall or across the ceiling. If your pet starts behaving in an unusual manner, listen closely or inspect the area the pet is looking at.

If you've just moved into a new home, this can be as stressful on your pets as it is on you. Give your pet a few weeks to see if its behavior changes as it adapts to the new surroundings.

If your pet's behavior changes drastically, or for a prolonged period of time, there could be a physiological reason. Make an appointment with your veterinarian for a checkup, including blood work. Many times a health-related problem will cause your pet to act in an unusual manner.

My four cats and two dogs always pick up some kind of paranormal activity way before I do. The dogs might stare at a particular spot and wag their tails and/or bark; the cats might take a defensive posture and make all their hair stand on end and hiss before racing from the room to another part of the house. I call my animals my early warning system, and if you are experiencing paranormal activity and notice your animals acting strangely just before or during the activity, make a note of it.

Moving Objects

In some cases, papers may fly off a desk, and plates or other items on a table or counter may slide off onto the floor. Pictures may fall off the wall, and so forth.

These types of events are generally experienced first-hand, and having a witness will add credibility to this type of occurrence.

Look for drafts if you're experiencing papers or other light objects flying off desks or other surfaces. Open windows or doors, ceiling fans, or someone walking by can cause such events.

Also ensure the desk or other surface is level. Sometimes, even someone walking across the room will set off vibrations that could make objects seem to move on their own.

Poltergeists are known for their ability to move objects and send them flying across a room. While poltergeists are one of the most common types of ghosts, they are also the hardest to get rid of.

Some paranormal investigators will use what are called *era cues* to incite this type of activity in order to determine what type of ghost is present in a home or other location.

Era cues are objects that the suspected ghost would be familiar with. For example, if it is thought that the ghost may be that of a child, a paranormal investigator may set out a ball or other toy for the ghost to interact with, as well as make sure a video camera is pointing at the ball the entire time. This ensures that no one living is tampering with the ball, and the camera will record any type of paranormal activity in order to confirm the presence of a ghost or other type of entity.

In other cases, a ghost may want something put in a place it thinks it belongs. For example, our first house had been in the family since it was built. My great-grandmother was an artist, and I have a few of her paintings. When we moved into the house, I hung one of her paintings over the fireplace and another one on the wall behind the sofa.

I was busy in another part of the house. When I walked back into the living room, the paintings were switched—the painting I'd hung over the sofa was now over the fireplace, and the fireplace painting was over the sofa. At first I didn't think anything of it, and switched the paintings back to where I'd originally hung them and went about my business.

A little while later I returned to the living room, and, you guessed it, the paintings were once again reversed. Being the only one home at the time, it finally dawned on me that one of the ghosts was switching the paintings around. I called my mother and asked her about this.

She confirmed that my great-grandmother, when alive, had hung the paintings in the exact spot the ghost kept moving them to. That explained why the paintings of hers were switched around. I gave in and hung the paintings the way the ghost of my great-grandmother wanted them. The pictures were never moved again.

This example doesn't mean the house was haunted by my great-grandmother—because other than switching the paintings, she really never showed up again as far as I know.

Shadows

Have you ever seen movement or something out of the corner of your eye, turned around, and nothing's there? Or maybe you've seen the shadow of something or someone scurry out of sight at a great rate of speed.

Shadows can appear in a vague human shape or size, but may also be larger or smaller, or have a less defined shape. It is possible you may see a shadow move around a room.

Many paranormal researchers call them *shadow people*, and not much is known about them.

I hesitate to call them ghosts because shadow people tend to be darker and their shape more obscure, although some people have reported seeing shadow people with red eyes.

Some researchers think they may be demons or another type of entity because of the dark appearance and malevolent feelings that can sometimes accompany them.

Still others believe they are "watchers" that are simply observing the activity around them for some unknown purpose. Shadow people can and do move very rapidly, especially if they've been spotted by you. They may appear to move faster than the speed of light. Fascinating.

There can be many causes for shadows. When you see a shadow, pay attention to your surroundings. Did a car just go down the street and its headlights cause a shadow to appear? Did a person or pet walk by a light, casting a shadow into the room or onto a wall? Look for obvious and not-so-obvious causes.

Sometimes when we see things out of the corners of our eyes, it's just our mind playing tricks on us or an optical illusion. Generally this is the case; however, there are times when a shadow person is lurking in the vicinity.

For instance, one evening as I was watching television, my dogs started barking at the staircase. I glanced in that direction and saw the shadow of a man coming down the stairs. I could even make out his fingers wrapped around the white stair railing. When the shadow person realized he'd been spotted, he darted at the speed of light down the stairs and disappeared. I didn't feel threatened or scared by his presence, as I felt he meant no harm.

In fact, shadow people fascinate me tremendously, and I wish he would show up more often so I could learn more about them. I've always found them to be rather complacent and to possess a rather interesting sense of humor.

One night while investigating a historic barn, I was up in the loft with several of my paranormal investigation team members. We were staring into the pitch blackness on the opposite end of the loft because we thought we saw something move and were trying to determine whether it was a ghost or a critter.

Anyway, I thought one of my team members was standing next to me because I saw a very dark, shadowy outline of a man. I reached out to touch his arm to ask him if he just saw something, but my hand went through the shadow and then the shadow disappeared. So what we'd been looking for was standing right next to me the entire time! I definitely have to admit that did creep me out a bit, and the shadow person repeated this activity with me twice more that same evening.

I'm still not exactly sure what to make of my encounter with the shadow people I've run across. Normally if there's a spirit in a room I can sense it the second I enter the space, but with shadow people I don't sense them until after I've already seen them and they have left the room. So what I'm sensing then is the residual energy they've left behind. Very strange.

Maybe one day science and paranormal research will be able to explain the secrets shadow people are hiding.

Physical Attacks or Being Touched

Being physically attacked by a spirit is extremely uncommon, but there have been reports of people being slapped, scratched, pushed, shoved, and grabbed by something or someone unseen.

The sensation of being touched or suffering physical attacks from a ghost are extremely rare. If you are being touched in a nonthreatening way, it's possible that a loved one who has passed is simply expressing affection.

The feeling of a hand on your shoulder or another part of your body, someone stroking your hair, or being touched or caressed in a nonviolent, nonthreatening manner all fall under this category. While disturbing and often frightening, you're not being harmed in any way.

This is quite different from suffering a bite, scratch, shove, or push from a ghost. That type of spirit means you harm, while a spirit that touches your shoulder or caresses your hair is simply trying to get your attention.

When my parents died, my daughter moved into their condo for a short period of time. She got sick and was lying on the couch. She felt a cool hand touch her forehead, obviously checking to see if she had a fever. My daughter told me she thought it was her grandpa, because he used to do that to her when he was alive and she wasn't feeling well.

This type of gesture on the part of a spirit is a gentle, loving way of connecting with family members who are still living, to show that the spirit's love transcends death.

If this type of event happens to you or a member of your family, there is no need to be alarmed or scared. Take comfort in the presence of a beloved family member or friend who has passed on.

Now, that's not to say that if a ghost tries to push or shove you down a flight of stairs, or bites and scratches you, that the ghost's motivations are pure, because they're not. If any spirit becomes physically violent without a good motivation behind those actions, it's time to get professional help to assist you.

It's possible a spirit will act out in other ways as well. As an example, we once had a spirit that took a particular disliking to one of my friends. Every time she went into the bathroom, the spirit would hold the door closed, trapping her.

There wasn't a lock on the bathroom door, so we couldn't attribute the activity to that, and she was the only person who ever got trapped in the bathroom.

I had to order the spirit to release the door to get my friend out of there! While I found this spirit's antics particularly amusing, my friend did not. This type of activity would also fall under other evidence. By *other evidence*, as I will explain in more detail a bit later in this chapter, I mean any type of activity that does not fit into one specific category as described in this book, or that could fit into multiple categories.

Apparitions

Ghosts and spirits have been known to manifest themselves in a variety of different manners.

The most commonly reported is a white, vaporous mist. Light and wispy, it could float in place or across a room. The mist may or may not take a definite human shape.

Ghosts have been known to partially appear. For example, you may see a head, hand, or set of legs.

A full-body apparition is normally not an everyday event. A ghost can appear transparent or semi-solid in form. You may even be able to see specific articles of clothing or facial features.

Ghosts have been known to appear only for a moment before fading away into nothingness, or linger and slowly dissipate. They may even disappear the instant you enter a room or after you've been in the room for a while.

It's next to impossible to predict when, where, or if a ghost will manifest.

For example, I was in an old historical house giving a tour of the home to a group of people. Since I knew the history of the house and the family who built it, I did the tour as a favor to the local historical society.

Anyway, we were on the third floor getting ready to head up the small, narrow flight of stairs to the cupola. There were about thirty of us in a single-file line due to the narrowness of the staircase. As we were walking up the stairs, a white, misty figure of a man appeared at the top of the stairs. I immediately knew it was the spirit of James, the son of the original owner of the home, but I kept talking in hopes no one would notice.

The white figure then began to slowly descend the stairs. Everyone stopped talking and flattened themselves against the wall to let the figure pass. At the figure descended, you could feel the cold emanating from it as it passed you. When the mist reached the bottom of the stairs, it simply disappeared. One of the people asked me what that was, and I told them it was the ghost of James and perfectly harmless. Fifteen people raced down three flights of stairs and out of the house, vowing never to set foot in it again.

Oh well, it's all what you're used to, I guess.

Other Evidence

You could experience unexplained writing on walls or paper, as well as footprints, handprints, and the like. If you have children, check to make sure they didn't write on the wall or put a dirty handprint on a counter, wall, or other object. Generally there is a very logical explanation for this type of evidence, but sometimes . . . not so much.

My paranormal investigation team and I were conducting training in one of the local cemeteries one night in late December. One of the team members and I split off from the rest of the team and began to walk up to one of the gravesites that has fascinated us for a number of years.

Anyway, as we walked through the crunchy snow, we kept hearing other footsteps close by us and assumed it was some of the other team members walking through the snow a little distance away from us.

As we got closer to the grave, we walked close to one of the street lights that illuminated the front gates of the cemetery. We commented on the footsteps and stopped and quickly turned around to see footstep impressions being made in the snow a short distance behind us, but no one was there. As soon as whatever ghost was walking behind us realized it had been discovered, the footsteps stopped.

The ghost following us didn't mean any harm. Perhaps it was just curious as to why people were roaming around the cemetery in the middle of the night . . . I mean, let's face it, it's not an everyday occurrence.

Conclusion

As you can see, there are many possibilities when it comes to the symptoms of a haunted house, or a home with paranormal activity being experienced. With those symptoms come many possible logical explanations to the activity.

Please note: just because you are experiencing some activity does not mean your home is haunted. It's not uncommon for some type of occasional paranormal activity to occur at one time or another. If the paranormal activity is consistent, however, it could be the sign of a real haunting.

Look for a logical explanation to any activity. It's normal to be scared or shaken up by these types of events. Try to remain calm and take a proactive stance in an effort to determine the cause of any activity.

CHAPTER 2

A Brief History of Ghosts

When people think of the word *ghost*, they think of an apparition. This is the common perception. In reality, though, the word *ghost* means the soul or spirit of a person who is deceased.

There have been reports of ghost ships, ghastly phantom marching armies, and ghost trains still heading to an unknown destination. While most of these sightings can probably be attributed to residual energy, some of them may not be so easy to dismiss.

The English word *ghost* is from the Old English word *gast* by way of the Germanic and Old Teutonic *gaisto-z*.

Linguists believe the pre-Germanic root word could have been *ghoizdo-z*, meaning "anger" or "fury."

The Old English word was used interchangeably with the Latin word *spiritus* (which originally meant "breath" or "blast") and is from the ninth century. It could also denote a good or bad spirit, such as an angel or demon, or the spirit of God or the Holy Ghost.

The meaning of the word *ghost* that we use today didn't show up until about the fourteenth century.

The idea of supernatural beings such as ghosts, demons, or gods and goddesses is shared by all human cultures and dates back tens of thousands of years, showing up in some cultures as ancestor worship.

Ghosts show up quite frequently in the religions of ancient Mesopotamia and were believed to have been created when someone dies, complete with the memories and mannerisms of the person who had died. The ancient Mesopotamians also believed that these ghosts would travel to another world and lead a life similar to that of people who were still alive. When someone got sick, the Mesopotamians often blamed the illness on a ghost or on one of their gods or demons.

In ancient Egypt there was a very widespread belief in the existence of ghosts; this belief was an integral part of ancient Egyptian culture. The beliefs about what happened to a person after they died changed almost constantly. The ancient Egyptians were so taken with the belief in spirits and the afterlife that they wrote about them in tomb paintings and inscriptions.

Cultures that participated in ancestor worship would hold rituals and rites to prevent the dead from coming back to harm them. Many of these cultures believed, and some still believe to this day, that their ancestors may be vengeful spirits who are envious of the living.

Some of the rituals of these cultures could include sacrifice, providing the deceased with food and drink, or banishment through magic. Many cultures bound the dead in an effort to keep them from coming back as spirits.

There are even cultures that "store" their dead chiefs and leaders in caves or on poles and keep them away from their villages, except for once a year when they are brought into the center of the village and a huge feast and ceremony are held in their honor. These societies believe that, by including the dead leaders of their village, the spirits of the dead will be appeased and not bring tragedy or bad times to the living villagers.

The human soul in many cultures is depicted as a bird or other animal; most cultures believed that the soul of a deceased person would return as an exact replica of the person's body in every way, even down to the type of clothing the person wore. This belief is often depicted in the artwork or writings of these cultures, such as in the Egyptian Book of the Dead.

Ghosts have appeared everywhere around the world and show up in many of our most revered texts. Ghosts appear in the Torah and the Holy Bible.

In the New Testament of the Bible, Jesus has to convince his Disciples that he is not a ghost. In addition, the church has been known to teach that many ghosts are really demons and that these demons are there to deceive us and turn us away from God.

Many Christians believe that orbs, a common paranormal occurrence, can be explained by saying that Satan can disguise himself as an angel of light.

Ghosts also appear in classic works such as Homer's *Odyssey* and *Iliad*, in which they were described as "a vapor, gibbering and whining into the earth." Homer's ghosts did not interact with the living very often, but they were called upon occasionally to give advice or a prophecy. They were not feared.

It wasn't until around the fifth century BCE that Greek ghosts started to haunt, scare people, and be either good or evil. The dead were mourned through public rituals that included sacrifice and food. The families of the deceased would invite the ghosts of their ancestors, but at the end of the ritual these "guests" were also invited to leave until the next year.

In medieval Europe, ghosts were considered to be either the souls of the dead or demons. The souls of the deceased returned for a specific reason, while the demons' only purpose was to torment and tempt the living.

* According to medieval writings, the living could tell a demon from a deceased person's soul by demanding that a ghost reveal its reason for being there in the name of Jesus Christ. The deceased person would reveal the reason, while a demon would have been banished at the sound of Jesus's name.

Accounts written in this era tell of people being restrained by ghosts until a priest could come and hear confession. Tales of ghostly armies fighting in the forests at night or in the remains of an Iron Age fort were not uncommon.

The Renaissance period in Europe gave rise to a great interest in the paranormal, and a number of writers, clergy, and others became dismayed at the fascination with what they thought were the "dark arts."

The Spiritualist movement, which started in the middle of the nineteenth century, saw a rise in popularity and interest in the paranormal. Hundreds of books were published about ghosts. Books like *Mysteries*, by Charles Elliott, contained accounts of spirits and spiritual beings, as well as an account of the Salem witch trials. *The Night Side of Nature*, by Catherine Crowe, was one of the first books to provide definitions of apparitions, haunted houses, and other types of ghosts.

Spiritual groups sprung up all across the world in the nineteenth century. The London Spiritualist Alliance published a newspaper about the paranormal called *The Light*.

Not to be outdone by the publications of many of the spiritual organizations, daily newspapers such as the *Chicago Daily Tribune* treated tales of ghosts and spirits as they did any other news story.

In 1882, the Society for Psychical Research was founded and set up committees to investigate claims of the paranormal.

The Spiritualist movement of the nineteenth century is still alive and well, even today, and has fueled people's interest in the paranormal. The ability to take photographs of ectoplasm and other spirit photography seemed to give legitimacy to the paranormal because scientific methods were being employed to study it. This line of thinking continues forward to modern times as well.

Throughout the last century, Hollywood has embraced the paranormal and given us such classics as *The Ghost and Mrs. Muir*, *The Uninvited*, *Dead of Night*, *Poltergeist*, *Field of Dreams*, *A Nightmare on Elm Street*, and so many others. Horror films and other movies dealing with the paranormal are, of course, still big box-office draws.

Hollywood isn't the only place that demons or other terrible creatures have shown up in history. Many different religions refer to evil spirits as demons or fallen angels.

Every religious group views demons or evil spirits in different ways. It would appear that in most religions there is good and evil, and the evil spirits are the most feared. People can become worried about possession, protecting themselves and their families, and concerned about these evil creatures that are doomed to walk the earth doing anything in their power to corrupt humanity and then disappear after they have wreaked havoc in someone's life.

In Christianity, evil spirits are traditionally viewed as fallen angels who were thrown out of heaven during the angel wars. Many Christians believe that because these fallen angels are never allowed to return to heaven, they are destined to walk the earth forever as punishment.

In Hinduism, evil spirits are seen as people who have committed terrible acts while alive, and when they die, their soul becomes an evil spirit. These evil spirits are destined to battle demigods forever.

Jinns, from Arab folklore, can be either good or evil. Jinns do not fight humans or attack them, but coexist alongside people.

Scientists have gotten into the act and have come up with many theories in an attempt to explain paranormal phenomena. For example, Professor Michael Persinger of Laurentian University in Canada speculates that the changes in the earth's geomagnetic fields may affect our brain lobes in such a way as to produce the experiences that we associate with a ghost or haunting.

Experiments conducted based on this theory have shown that stimulation of the temporal lobe with certain magnetic fields can elicit experiences common to the activity in a haunting, but this theory is highly controversial.

Other scientists have speculated that sound, especially infrasound, can cause people to experience emotions such as anxiety, sadness, the feeling of being watched, and so forth.

This theory is close to the "fear cage" theory that involves electromagnetic fields. Science has shown that high levels of electromagnetic energy can cause people to have the feeling of being watched, hallucinations, and the like. However, it is possible to eliminate the presence of an electromagnetic field quite easily through the use of an electromagnetic detector, which is a common tool for paranormal investigators.

Science is making advances all the time, and new and better ghost-hunting equipment is rapidly making its way into the hands of the general public. This equipment is transforming the way paranormal researchers are gathering evidence to prove the existence of ghosts.

Even with the advances that have been made thus far, the debate still rages on about the existence of ghosts—as it has done for centuries and will probably continue to do in the future. However, if other people could experience what I have seen, and what many of you are experiencing or have experienced, most skeptics would be left with little doubt as to the existence of the paranormal.

CHAPTER 3

What Kind of Haunting Is It?

A *haunting* is defined by Dictionary.com as "an act of a person or thing that haunts; a visitation." The word *haunt* means "to inhabit, visit, or appear in the form of a ghost or other supernatural being."

Yet these dictionary definitions are not quite accurate. Just because you are experiencing paranormal activity does not mean your house is haunted.

There are many possible types of hauntings, but paranormal researchers generally agree on three main classifications. While some people confuse some kinds of ghosts as a type of haunting, I don't believe this to be the case at all. There are far more types of ghosts than types of hauntings.

In this chapter we're going to explore the three main types of haunting and their general characteristics. As I've said before, and it bears repeating, no two real hauntings are alike, but they will share some common denominators.

I want to take a few moments to dispel some common misconceptions people have when it comes to a haunting. First of all, not all hauntings are caused by demons. I can't for the life of me figure out why some people automatically jump to this conclusion. A demonic haunting is extremely rare and will be discussed later in this chapter.

Second, not every house or building is built on top of sacred or ancient burial grounds. In reality, there are very few homes or buildings that have this distinction, and many of those have no paranormal activity at all.

I've investigated many homes that are near Native American burial grounds and in areas once inhabited by Native Americans, and none of the paranormal activity associated with these homes could be attributed to the Native Americans who once occupied the area.

That being said, let's explore the three main types of haunting that can and do occur in homes and businesses across the world.

Residual Haunting

A *residual haunting* is thought to be the imprint of a past event. Although most times a residual haunting is linked to a tragic event, it can also be a very mundane routine that was repeated often in life, such as walking up stairs.

A residual haunting does not involve a ghost at all, and is presumed to be a form of energy that remains in a specific location. A tragic event, or an activity repeated many times, seems to be caught in a time warp and is then replayed over and over. Think of a residual haunting as a movie or videotape that keeps playing continuously.

If you are experiencing a residual haunting, you may see people, animals, or other objects interacting with the environment the way it was sometime in the past. It's also quite possible to hear footsteps or notice a fragrance lingering in the air.

Although similar in many ways to an intelligent haunting, in a residual haunting there is no attempt at interaction or communication with the living. For example, a residual haunting is not going to turn lights on or off.

You could have a residual haunting if the activity only occurs on certain days and times, and if there is no attempt to communicate or interact with the living.

Residual hauntings can't be stopped or made to go away. In some cases, they will begin to fade over a long period, stop altogether, or continue forever. A residual haunting, while sometimes unnerving and often very frightening, is totally harmless.

Strange noises you hear in your home may be the result of a residual haunting. An example: my great-grandfather built the first house my husband and I lived in when we got married. Every spring we'd suffer through being woken up at about four a.m. by something loud crashing to the basement floor. My husband and I would jump out of bed and rush downstairs only to find nothing out of place.

I asked my father about the noise, and he chuckled and said that his grandfather was a mushroom farmer and the horse-drawn plow he used was suspended from the ceiling in the basement. During plowing season in the spring, he would let it fall to the floor and then hook it up to the waiting horses outside the huge window in the basement. The horses would then pull the plow out the window and into the fields. This is a classic case of a residual haunting. There wasn't a ghost, just this routine activity repeating itself over and over.

Other examples of residual hauntings are the replay of a death scene on the anniversary of someone's death or footsteps heard on a floor or stairway every night, which could be the repeating of a previous owner's bedtime routine.

Energy from past events can also be recorded into stone, wood, and other materials. If building materials from old structures are recycled into new construction, as sometimes happens, the residual energy from past events can manifest itself in the form of perceived paranormal activity in the new buildings.

One such case was that of the foundation stones of an old Civil War hospital and barracks being incorporated into a new building. Once this building was completed and occupied, many people who worked there reported seeing Civil War soldiers walking around, as well as hearing moans, screams, and the sounds of marching or heavy boots walking down some of the hallways.

Was this new building haunted? Of course not; it was simply the residual energy of the traumatic events of the Civil War being replayed over and over again because of the use of the old stones in the construction of the building. You see, the energy of events can be stored in anything relatively porous—in this case, the stones from the old building.

Traditional/Intelligent Haunting

This type of haunting is normally what people think of when they hear the word *ghost*. Yet an intelligent haunting is rare.

There are many reasons a spirit could be haunting a certain location: for example, a spirit is tied to the site or a certain person; a spirit died there as a result of a traumatic event such as a murder, car accident, and so on; or the spirit might have some unfinished business or task they feel compelled to complete before moving on to the other side. In some cases, spirits could have died suddenly or in their sleep and not even realize they are dead.

Some spirits might be held here by living relatives or friends who are so emotionally upset by the death that they can't let go of the one who has passed and allow the spirit to cross over. In some instances, it is the spirit who is tied to the loved one and does not want to let go.

This particular scenario is one of the hardest to deal with. There's a fine line between holding onto a person after they've passed and just keeping that person in your memories. In most cases, the one holding the spirit here doesn't even realize what he or she is doing, and that this unwillingness to let go is causing distress to the spirit of the loved one who has passed away.

When someone dies, it is very important that the person go into the light and cross over to the other side. The alternative is becoming an earthbound spirit because the loved ones the person left behind cannot bear to let go.

Please don't misunderstand me. It is of course perfectly normal to mourn the death of someone you loved and cared about, but, like everything else, it can be carried to the extreme, and actually cause not only emotional distress to the living but to the dead as well. In other words, not being able to let go is not healthy emotionally or physically for the living, and can also cause harm to the spirit of the person who died.

An intelligent haunting could also be caused by spirits not wanting to cross over because of some injustice they feel was done to them. Or they may not want to face judgment on the other side for things they've done in their lives. In some cases, they may believe they cannot cross over because they are protecting some secret.

An intelligent haunting is generally associated with lots of physical activity. This activity may include slamming, opening, closing, and unlocking doors and windows; voices; and sounds. More rarely, a strong presence, scent, or touch can occur. It's even possible to see a spirit in the form of a mist or a full-body or partial-body apparition.

The main difference between an intelligent haunting and a residual haunting is that in the former the spirit will interact in some way with the living and/or be aware of its surroundings. The ghost may be responsive to, and may go out of its way to interact with, the living. Moreover, objects might be moved, and paranormal events can occur in response to a request by the people living in the home or a paranormal investigator.

Three types of spirits are possible in an intelligent haunting: benevolent, benign, and malevolent.

A *benevolent spirit* will be kind-hearted. They might seek to assist or protect the living. Some benevolent spirits will protect the living from an evil spirit or other types of danger.

One night I was awakened by something shaking me. I could feel the hands on my shoulders, and I was being shaken very violently. When I woke up, I noticed the house was very cold. I checked the thermostat and realized our old oil furnace had gone out. I woke up my husband, and we quickly determined that we needed to call an emergency repair service. In the meantime, my husband turned off the valve feeding oil to the furnace. When the repairman got there, he told us that had I not woken up and noticed the heat was out, the house could have exploded because of the problem with our furnace.

While I never did figure out the identity of the ghost who woke me up that night, I owe the ghost my life and the lives of my family.

A *benign spirit* will not be concerned with the living and instead will just go about its business. This type of spirit is difficult to classify; it could be part of either a residual haunting or an intelligent haunting.

When my grandmother passed away, her house was sold to a nice young couple who were purchasing their first home. A few weeks after they bought the house, they called my parents and told them that things were being thrown off the top of the refrigerator and the window blinds in the living room were being raised and lowered at certain intervals during the day. Quite frankly, they were scared.

My mother called me and told me to "fix it." You have to love moms. On my way over to the house, my mind wandered back to the days I spent with my grandmother and to where she kept various items in the house when she lived there.

I was met at the door by a very anxious and very terrified couple. I assured them that my grandmother was a gentle woman who meant them no harm. I explained to them that my grandmother kept her pills on top of the refrigerator and detested taking medication, and that at certain times of the day she would raise or lower the front window shades to either let in or block out the sun.

I calmly stood in the middle of the living room and said, "Grandma, it's okay. You don't have to take those nasty pills anymore, and this nice young couple live in the house now and plan on raising a family just like you did. They have promised to take very good care of your home. So I need you to go join Grandpa. Walk into the light, Grandma. I love you."

Within a few minutes, the air in the house became lighter, and the couple lived there many more years without further incident.

So while my grandmother did cause obvious activity, she didn't interact with the living. She simply went about her business as she would have done had she still been alive; only in death could she show her frustration with her medication by throwing anything on top of the refrigerator onto the floor.

A *malevolent spirit* is an entity whose only goal is to inflict harm on the living. This type of ghost could just be an angry spirit or a negative spirit; or it could be demonic or inhuman. More on this type of haunting is discussed on the following pages.

Negative-Entity Haunting or Infestation

A negative-spirit haunting is almost always malevolent and often involves an entity that is "inhuman," meaning that it has never been alive in human form. Such spirits are very unfriendly in nature. This type of haunting can initially behave like an intelligent haunting, but will quickly escalate and become almost overpowering.

A demonic or negative-entity haunting will generally begin in a place where people are suffering from great emotional duress or stress due to psychological or emotional problems, or in a home in which someone is addicted to drugs or alcohol.

Many paranormal researchers believe that demons and other negative entities feed on the emotional upheaval, since a weak person is easier to take advantage of and control.

A negative entity—be it a demon, elemental, or another type of angry spirit—appears to hold resentment or envy toward the living.

Some paranormal researchers feel that negative spirits like demons or elementals have to be summoned or invited by a living person before they can take up residence. A person can invite such ghosts and not even be conscious of doing so. A séance, Ouija board, or the form of fortunetelling called *scrying* can all unintentionally summon a negative spirit, and it is possible for one to have been summoned a number of years ago and still be present in a location. Unless you know how to properly protect yourself from any type of negative entity—and know how to properly scry, hold a séance, and use a Ouija board—you shouldn't use these forms of spirit communication.

Someone who has passed away and was not at all a nice person in life may return and be a very negative, nasty ghost. Such a spirit would also fall into this category, because its only goal is to make life miserable for the living—just as was the case in life.

Here's an example. My team and I investigated a case in which two people believed that their ex-landlord, whom we'll call "Frank," was haunting their home. From what I understand, Frank was not a nice person in life, so there was no reason to expect him to have changed his personality in death.

Anyway, I went into the home and began provoking the spirit—not something I normally do, and not something I would recommend to anyone who isn't confident in handling an angry ghost. I accused Frank of being afraid of a woman, and asked him why, if he was this big, tough guy, was he running away from a girl? I took it pretty far. I called him a coward and emasculated him pretty terribly.

After about an hour of this, I asked the homeowner if I could get access to the attic. Often a ghost will hide in order to avoid detection. The homeowner told me he would unscrew the access panel in the ceiling and let me up into the space.

We'd been using a tape recorder looking for EVPs (electronic voice phenomena, or ghost voices), and upon playback after the investigation we heard a voice we couldn't identify say, "No, don't go up there."

I went up into the attic with a tape recorder and digital camera and began taking pictures and once again calling Frank out. After getting no response, I said, "Fine. I don't know what you want me to do," and I went out of the attic.

Upon playing back the tape from the recorder I'd left in the attic for a period of time, we heard the same unidentified voice say, "Frank is here." After I'd said I didn't know what he wanted me to do, the same voice said, "Die."

Just so you know, we did attempt to get that spirit out of the house using some of the methods described later on in this book. I can't say for sure that what we did worked. Although a few months later, the family reported that the activity had stopped.

Provoking a ghost is not recommended unless you know exactly what you're doing. Many paranormal investigators often provoke a ghost to elicit a response. We do this because until we can get some type of activity or evidence to evaluate, we can't state with any great amount of certainty what type of ghost or haunting we are dealing with.

Provoking a spirit is not something anyone other than a trained paranormal investigator should do . . . ever! The reason is this: there are some types of entities that draw energy from your anger, frustration, and fear. These are all negative emotions, and they can make an entity stronger and more powerful.

When I or any member of my team provoke a spirit, we do it in a specific way, and we know when to stop provoking so as to not make the entity either stronger or cause more terror for the family living in the home.

Conclusion

It is important to distinguish the type of haunting you are experiencing, as some of them are curable and some are not.

Just like people, there are good spirits and bad spirits. Remember: most spirits were once in a human body. It has been my experience that most spirits want to be acknowledged in some way, which is why they act out. They do it to get your attention!

Once you've defined the type of haunting you have, the next goal is to identify the type of ghost or spirit you are dealing with.

CHAPTER 4

Types of Ghosts

There are many types of ghosts, and the appearance of certain types of ghosts does not mean your house is haunted; it may instead only be experiencing a bout of paranormal activity. Certain standards must be met for a house to be considered haunted. First, the activity must be consistent, and, second, the ghost needs to make an attempt at interacting with humans. So, while some paranormal activity may occur in your home once in a while, such activity does not necessarily mean your house is haunted.

Paranormal researchers and ghost hunters alike have broken down the types of spirits into a ridiculous number of subcategories. The types of ghosts and/or entities listed in this chapter can be divided into many subcategories, but generally they will behave in certain ways depending on the type of ghost they are.

Defining the type of ghost or spirit that is causing a paranormal event is one of the most important factors, because it determines the method(s) that can be used to rid your home of any unwanted ghost or spirit. (For the difference between ghosts and spirits, see chapter 8.)

Poltergeists

Poltergeist is German for "noisy ghost," and that's exactly what this type of spirit is: very noisy. A poltergeist also has the greatest ability to affect the world of the living.

They can bang on walls and doors, create the sound of footsteps, and play music. They can steal and hide our possessions at will, only to return them later—usually in a different place. They slam doors, turn lights on and off, flush toilets, and have been known to throw things across rooms with a violent force. They can break household objects, such as plates and glasses, destroy clothes, and throw stones, rocks, and dirt. Poltergeists have also been known to pull people's hair and tug on clothing, and the more malevolent poltergeists can slap, scratch, and push people.

Some poltergeists are capable of producing voices, screams, explosions, and scratches. Some can cause beds to shake violently.

They can make puddles of water appear out of nowhere, make telephones and doorbells ring, and even cause physical injury.

To put it bluntly, many poltergeists are not very friendly and can make your life a living hell.

Poltergeists don't typically communicate or even attempt to communicate with the living, don't show any particular attachment to the location they are haunting, and are often the most difficult type of ghost to get rid of because it is almost impossible to determine what they want, if anything. While they can cause a great amount of damage, most poltergeists don't try to harm the living intentionally.

However, some poltergeists are so malevolent that they've been classified as demons by paranormal researchers.

I know that sounds contradictory, but it really all depends on the "personality" of the poltergeist. A mild-tempered poltergeist may only make minor mischief by taking car keys and rapping on walls, while a particularly nasty and aggressive poltergeist can turn the contents of a home topsy-turvy!

Yet many paranormal investigators feel that teenagers or people who are overly emotional can unwittingly cause poltergeist activity. The theory is that the increased level of emotional distress or energy feeds the poltergeist, allowing it to act.

A possible way to determine if a poltergeist is real or being manifested involuntarily through a living person is to take particular notice of when the activity occurs.

For example, if the poltergeist activity only occurs when a teenager or other person under extraordinary stress is present, or the activity seems more focused on that person, then the more likely it is that the poltergeist activity is being unconsciously generated by that person.

If that's the case, once the teenager matures, or the stress level is decreased, the activity will stop. The problem is that the teenager who unwittingly caused the activity may be left with deep feelings of guilt. It is important to explain that the events were not their fault in any way and were due to circumstances beyond their control.

You know your teenager better than anyone, and if you feel your teenager may need some psychological counseling, then by all means get him or her any and all help that is needed.

It's important to note that just because the poltergeist activity appears to be centered around one person, it doesn't mean that person is causing the activity—but it is definitely worth taking a closer look at. For example, if you suspect that a person in your home who is stressed out could be inadvertently causing poltergeist-type activity, then whenever the activity occurs, take note of who was present and each person's mood.

If the activity only occurs when a certain person is present, it could be one of two things: either this person is unknowingly causing the activity because he or she is over-emotional or that particular person is being haunted. It's very possible that a person can be haunted and that a spirit has attached itself to the person in some fashion. It could be the spirit of a loved one who has passed away that has attached itself to a family member, or, in some cases, the ghost could be attracted to that person for some reason.

The most important thing to remember when dealing with poltergeists is to be calm but firm in how you approach them. It's important not to show anger, fear, or any type of aggression toward them, but instead to let them know in no uncertain terms that you are in control not only of yourself but also the situation.

An example: a few years ago I ran across a particularly aggressive poltergeist on an investigation. I arrived at the house and was greeted at the door by the homeowners. The instant I walked through the door, a knife came out of nowhere and lodged itself in the doorjamb next to me.

The homeowners were terrified, but I calmly reached up and pulled the knife out of the doorjamb and asked the poltergeist in a firm tone, "Is that the best you got?" The atmosphere of the house immediately changed and became less tense, and the air felt calmer.

I *do not* recommend that you challenge a poltergeist as I did in that situation. At that time I'd had years of experience dealing with this type of ghost, and felt confident in my ability to diffuse the situation and let the poltergeist know that I couldn't be intimidated and wasn't afraid of it.

You can let the poltergeist know that you are not afraid of it, but do it in a different manner than I did. For example, you can say in a firm, calm tone, "I know you are here, and I'm not afraid of you. This is my house, and your behavior is not acceptable. Please leave my house right now."

Notice that you are not challenging the ghost in any manner or provoking it in a way that could cause the poltergeist to escalate its activity. You are simply claiming your home as yours in a proactive manner.

Some poltergeists feed on negative emotions. Feelings of fear, anger, emotional distress, crying, and so forth can all add fuel to the poltergeist and make it stronger and more powerful. By dealing with poltergeists calmly but firmly, you are not empowering them. You are empowering yourself.

Spirits Out for Revenge

Some paranormal investigators call these types of spirits *avengers* or *revengers*. This type of ghost returns to right a wrong or avenge a death. In other words, it is seeking some type of justice.

For example, if a person is the victim of a murder and the killer hasn't been caught, the victim's spirit may return to reveal the murderer or extract some type of personal revenge against the attacker.

A while back, I came in contact with a spirit whose death had officially been ruled an accident. After speaking with this spirit for quite some time, it became apparent that her death was not an accident after all. It took a bit of talking on my part to convince this spirit that revenge was not the answer, and the only entity being hurt by this vengeance was herself.

Even though this entity had crossed over at death, she periodically came back in an attempt to exact revenge against those who she felt had caused her death. The question here is: would this spirit have exacted revenge if given half a chance? My guess would be yes. Would anything have been achieved by this? No.

Part of my job as a medium is to bridge this communication gap between the living and the dead and try to bring a situation to a conclusion that is fair for all parties concerned. By spending time talking with this spirit, I was able to convince the spirit that it was not up to her to exact revenge, that the person responsible for her death would eventually have to answer for it to a much higher power.

A ghost that is seeking revenge may appear at the scene of the crime until someone living understands that foul play may have occurred. The spirit may also make itself known to someone it knew and trusted while alive in order to get assistance in seeing that justice is served.

Spirits out for revenge feel that they've been wronged in some way while alive, and can behave in a vengeful and hostile manner.

These types of ghosts can be male or female, and it's possible they may appear in the same clothing they wore when they were alive.

In some cases they can appear as apparitions but can't speak and may try to communicate with the living through different means, such as appearing very often at the place they died or were killed. They may continue appearing to one or more living people they knew in life until that person or people realize that some type of foul play could have been involved in the death.

Such ghosts can cause cold spots in rooms and sudden drops in temperature. They may also act in the same manner as a poltergeist and throw objects around rooms, slam doors, and so on. In extreme cases, they can go much further. They can push people down stairs, in front of cars, or find any way possible to cause physical harm and/or emotional suffering to the person they feel has wronged them. When a vengeful spirit goes as far as to try to harm someone physically, it wouldn't be uncommon for this type of spirit to be mistaken for a demon.

Ghosts out for revenge only have one goal, and that's to make life as miserable as possible for the person or people who, for whatever reason, they feel deserve it.

A good fictional example of this is found in the 1990 movie *Ghost*. The ghost, played by Patrick Swayze, was determined not to leave until his murderer had been brought to justice, and he used whatever means necessary to accomplish this task.

Messengers

We've all heard stories about people seeing the vision of a loved one appear to them, only to find out later that the person died at that exact moment or soon after.

Also known as *crisis apparitions*, messengers appear as a vision to another living person, usually a loved one, even though they may be hundreds of miles apart.

Some messengers will appear to a loved one shortly after death to give the living person a message of some type—normally a message that they are okay, or to bring their loved one comfort.

A messenger might appear to a loved one in an attempt to convey a secret or to warn the living of some danger.

Messengers may appear over and over again until the living person understands what the ghost is trying to communicate.

The presence of a messenger is not a true haunting, but a paranormal event or series of events. Once the living person understands the message, it's more than likely that the messenger ghost will cross over and not appear again.

Messengers are generally translucent, and normally will appear to be wearing the same clothing they wore when they were alive.

Many messengers will haunt their graves and can be accompanied by a mist. They can be male or female, and most often will appear to someone they knew and trusted when they were alive.

Spirits That Haunt

These types of ghosts are extremely rare, and do constitute a true haunting.

Ghosts that haunt will hang around a place they loved while they were alive, or a place they just can't bear to say goodbye to.

This type of spirit may or may not interact with the living and is often mistaken for a residual haunting. Some of these types of spirits want to stay where they were the happiest when they were alive, or to protect a place or the people living or working in that place.

They may be human or inhuman in appearance, and will often be seen wearing the same clothing they wore when alive. They can be male or female, and generally will only haunt one particular location.

This type of haunting also follows a very specific pattern. There is a real sense that an actual personality is present and that the ghost is capable of thought and able to respond to or communicate with any living people present.

It's also possible that this type of spirit will only appear once, or it could appear many times.

One of the intelligent haunting cases I've worked on involved a ghost I'll call "Jacob." Jacob was the son of the original owner of the home, and the family was one of the most prominent families in the town during the mid-1800s.

This family was also very private and, from what I've been able to gather during the course of my research, had many secrets. Jacob refused to leave the house after he died because he believed someone had to protect the family secrets.

Jacob would hide tools, clomp loudly up and down the staircases, appear as a white mist and float past people, try to push people down the third-floor staircase, and basically do anything within his means to scare people out of what he perceived to still be his home and to protect the family secrets that were long forgotten by the living.

However, Jacob would also stop when requested to do so, and would return items he'd taken if you asked him nicely. In other words, Jacob was an intelligent ghost and would frequently interact with the living, whether it was to show his anger or frustration over the renovations or simply because he wanted human contact.

Other Common Types of Ghosts

Orbs

Orbs will mostly show up as transparent balls of light either floating above the ground or hovering in one place. When photographed, many orbs will look like a comet with a trail of light behind them indicating movement.

There is much controversy in the paranormal world about the validity of orbs. It's estimated that roughly 85 percent of apparent orbs are really a reflection, a speck of dust or dirt, or an insect. Even raindrops or moisture in the air can cause an orb-like anomaly to appear in photographs.

The appearance of orbs in a photograph or video can also be due to weather conditions and many other factors at the time the picture or video was taken.

Orbs can be anywhere: cemeteries, homes, vacant parcels of land, or at your local store. You can't see them, you can't feel them, but they may be there nonetheless.

When they show up in photographs, they generally appear as little balls of white light, although they can also be red, blue, pink, purple, or just about any other color. No one knows for sure just how many colors orbs are capable of producing.

If you look closely at some orbs, you will notice different patterns within the sphere itself. Like an intricately woven spider web, no two orbs are alike. In other orbs there appear to be faces. It's as if someone were looking at you through another dimension or a different place in time. There are a few theories as to what these mysterious balls of light actually are.

Some people believe orbs are remote viewers used by aliens from another planet. The theory is that because orbs are very rarely visible with the naked eye, aliens are able to watch the events occurring on Earth virtually undetected.

Followers of this hypothesis feel that through the use of orbs, aliens have discovered not only how to be stealthy in their movements but also how to use a very economical means of traveling through space or time.

Another theory is that the orbs are actually angelic beings watching over people on earth. Some believers of this theory feel that angels come to heal the sick, comfort people in times of need, or act as guardians to protect the weak.

The most popular theory is that orbs are spirits of the dead in their purest form. It is a belief among some paranormal researchers that spirits or ghosts are composed entirely of energy.

This theory does help explain why, when being photographed, more orbs appear in pictures taken with a flash than without one—energy reacts to energy.

So when it comes to orbs, the debate continues. Almost every paranormal researcher will acknowledge their existence, but not many will firmly state what they are.

Light Creatures or Light Beings

Light creatures, or light beings, are the most mysterious anomalies I've run across in my time as a paranormal researcher. No one is really quite sure what they are.

Some people think they are angels, while others think they are creatures from another dimension. Still others don't believe they are light beings at all, but rather light *rods*.

It has also been suggested that they could be a vortex or a portal opening or closing. A vortex or portal is the method by which some people think orbs, ghosts, spirits, and other beings travel from their dimension into ours.

There is no rhyme or reason to where light creatures show up or when; they just appear. When photographed, they show up as little bars of light or as a misshapen light form.

Apparitions

Catching an apparition on film is what every ghost hunter spends hours dreaming about, but seldom ever sees.

Apparitions can appear to be transparent or as a solid human form, and everything in between. Many people report seeing apparitions wearing clothing they would have worn when they were alive.

Most paranormal researchers agree that there are four classes of apparitions: *partial, invisible, visible,* and *solids.*

A partial apparition may appear to not have a complete body. A partial apparition could be missing a head, arms, or legs, or you may *only* see a head or a set of legs or arms.

An invisible apparition is a ghost that cannot be seen by the naked eye, but shows up on film or in a photograph.

A visible apparition will be able to be seen with the naked eye, but will appear transparent or translucent.

A solid apparition will look as real as you or I do, and many people mistake them for a real person—until the apparition vanishes right in front of their eyes.

Jacob, whom I spoke about earlier in this chapter, is a prime example of an apparition. He would very often appear as a white mist or cloud and move about the rooms scaring people half to death and send them fleeing from the house. I believe he enjoyed this activity immensely.

Anniversary Ghosts

As the name suggests, these types of spirits appear on an anniversary that had some significance for them when they were alive. This could be a death, birthday, or other similarly significant date.

For example, a spouse who has passed away may appear to her living mate on her birthday or on the couple's wedding anniversary.

These types of spirits are not residual, since they will acknowledge you in some way. For example, they may look right at you or attempt to speak to you in some manner. But seeing anniversary ghosts does not mean your house is haunted; this type of spirit will only appear once or twice a year and only to mark some special event.

Family Ghosts

These types of spirits seem to connect themselves to their families and will travel with them if they move. Many paranormal researchers believe that these types of entities can and will warn the living about a death or impending disaster.

It is also widely believed that if you ask your deceased relatives to take part in family photographs, they will appear in the pictures. I've seen this work and I've also seen it not work, so I suppose it's kind of a hit-or-miss situation, but definitely worth a try.

I was asked to advise on such a case a few years ago. An elderly widow lived in a huge Victorian house, and while it was way too big for her to keep up, she refused to move because she was afraid her husband who'd died long ago would not know where she was and wouldn't follow her to a new residence. Apparently, she believed that her husband came back to keep her company every once in a while, and, by all accounts, he probably did.

Unfortunately, or fortunately, whichever way you choose to look at it, the woman had a severe stroke and died before any decision was made on what would be the best course of action for her and the spirit of her husband. Either way, the case is resolved, and they are presumably together again on the other side.

Haunted Objects

In some cases, ghosts will haunt a particular object that they loved and cherished when they were alive. Have you ever been to an antique store and noticed that a piece of furniture or other item didn't "feel" right, and you didn't buy it because of that feeling? Chances are your instincts were correct and that object could have been haunted by its former owner.

Ghosts can attach themselves to almost anything, including a piece of jewelry, a doll, a chair or sofa, and so forth.

I got a call recently from a woman who had moved because of the paranormal activity in her home. Yet she was still experiencing the same type of activity in her new home, and after a lengthy conversation it became apparent that the ghost was not a nice one, and was terrorizing her, her husband, and their small children.

After asking her several questions, I learned that she had moved a mirror from her old house that had been there when they moved in—and had probably been in that house for a long period of time—to her new home.

Not only that, but she was etching the mirror with decorative designs. It also didn't take me long to figure out that the woman on the other end of the telephone was somewhat of an emotional basket case. So, by her being such an overly emotional person, and etching the mirror, her negative emotions were actually drawing this negative entity into her home!

I told her to get rid of the mirror immediately. While she was reluctant to do so, her husband grabbed the mirror off the wall, took it outside, and smashed it into a million pieces before putting it in the garbage.

The paranormal activity they'd been experiencing stopped immediately and never returned. It's important to understand that the negative spirit that came through the mirror only came through because of this woman's extreme emotions. The mirror was simply the easiest way for the spirit to come through. In fact, this woman was by accident summoning this negative entity and inviting it into her home. The mirror was only haunted because this woman unintentionally projected her negative emotions into the mirror.

You see, emotions are energy, and whether you are putting out good energy or negative energy all depends on your mood. If you are happy, laughing, feeling content and at peace, then you will be putting out positive energy and only positive energy will come to you.

If you are sad, angry, jealous, upset, or emotionally distraught, those are negative emotions and you will be putting out negative energy, so in return only negative things will be attracted to that energy.

A common belief among some paranormal researchers is that mirrors can act as a portal or door to the other side, and ghosts of all types, good and bad, can pass back and forth at will.

Now, before you run around your house removing every mirror in sight, keep in mind that while a mirror may act as a portal, in most cases something has to pull that ghost through the mirror. By this I mean that if a person is highly emotionally distraught, angry, sad, upset, and so on, the likelihood of an entity being pulled through the mirror may be increased.

Negative emotions are very powerful and could be strong enough to pull a negative ghost of any type through a mirror and into a house. Cases of this type of activity are extremely rare, and there is normally no real need for concern if you have mirrors in your home.

So your obvious question is: how many mirrors do I have in my own house, right? The answer is five, although that will be reduced by two as soon as I can convince my husband to replace the mirrored closet doors with regular bi-fold doors.

Historical Ghosts

Sometimes ghosts will attach themselves to a particular location, such as a battlefield. They will very rarely if ever interact with the living, and instead they just appear to go about their business as they did when they were alive. These types of ghosts will generally appear in period clothing or the clothing they wore while alive.

There has been much research done on Civil War battlefields, with many reports of tourists and visitors to the sites capturing what appeared to be Civil War soldiers still engaged in battle.

This would be an example of a historical ghost, and while much of this activity is probably due to residual haunting (see chapter 3), much of it cannot be explained away so easily.

Because of the energy left behind by a battle, it wouldn't be unusual for that energy to manifest itself in the form of soldiers still fighting a war. It does not mean that the spirits of these brave men and women are earthbound and still on the battlefield for all eternity. It simply means that because of the trauma associated with the event, the energy will keep playing the event over and over like a videotape playing in a continuous loop.

Hitchhiker Spirits or Traveling Ghosts

Ahhhh, these are the ghosts from which legends are born. The appearance of hitchhiker spirits may only happen on the anniversary of their death. When alive, they were killed while hitchhiking and will generally appear at that location only. This type of ghost will interact with the living and generally ask for a ride, but before you drop them off they will disappear from your vehicle.

A *traveling ghost* will normally stay on one particular road or along a specific route. Generally this is where they met their death due to a tragic accident. These types of ghosts are often found waiting to catch a train, airplane, bus, car, or even a horse.

More likely than not, a traveling ghost will only appear on the anniversary of its death, although they could appear at any time of the day or night.

The most famous of the hitchhiker ghosts is probably Resurrection Mary, who has been seen either just outside the gates of Resurrection Cemetery in Chicago or somewhere near the cemetery. The story goes that Mary is a beautiful young woman who stands on the corner of Archer Road. People, normally men, stop to pick her up and give her a ride. She gets in the back seat and gives the driver an address before falling silent. By the time the driver gets to the address, the woman has vanished.

Many versions of this story exist, and it is now somewhat of an urban legend in the Chicago area. One of the most famous of the stories goes like this:

A cab driver picked up a woman on a cold, dark night standing in front of a shopping center with no coat on. The cabbie reported that when he stopped, the woman jumped into the front seat of his cab. She was wearing a fancy white dress and appeared to be about twenty-one years old. The young woman sat and looked out the car window at the snow and only became animated a couple miles down the road when she said, "Here! Here!" The cabbie hit the brakes.

The cabbie looked around and didn't see a house. "Where?" he asked. And then the woman stuck out her arm and pointed across the road, "There!"

The driver looked to his left and saw a little shack, and when he turned around to face the woman she was gone. She had vanished, although the car door never opened.

Doppelgängers (Doubles)

A doppelgänger is the double of a living person or animal. These types of entities will appear as exact doubles of someone who is living, and are generally considered to be an omen of bad luck or a death omen. For example, someone may see a friend who lives miles away appear as a vision, and then find out later that this friend died either right before or right after the vision of the friend appeared.

In some cultures, the appearance of a doppelgänger seen by a person's friends or relatives tells of an illness or danger in the future, while seeing one's own doppelgänger is an omen of death. In Norse mythology, they are seen as a ghostly double that precedes a living person, often performing that person's actions in advance.

Ghosts with Purpose

These types of spirits seem to have returned for a specific reason, and normally it is something important that motivates this type of ghost to return after death.

For example, a dead parent or spouse could return to visit loved ones one last time, to reveal the location of an important document or money, or to warn of danger or an upcoming illness.

A ghost with purpose has a different reason for appearing than a ghost out for revenge, although it is common to use the two terms interchangeably. However, it has been my experience that a ghost with purpose is out to help the living or warn the living of some upcoming event. A ghost with purpose generally is a peaceful and gentle type of spirit, while a ghost out for revenge is often angry and is frequently mistaken for a negative entity.

An example of a ghost with purpose: I used to find objects that belonged to my great-aunt in the upstairs hallway of her old house soon after my husband and I moved in; I'd inherited many of her things and kept them around the house. The objects would be different every time, but they would always appear in the same spot.

My father was over fixing a few things around the house and I mentioned it to him. We trotted upstairs to investigate. My dad noticed that the floorboards were loose in the exact spot in the hallway where the objects had been appearing, and, after retrieving a screwdriver and hammer from the basement, he gently removed the loose floorboards with the intent of re-securing them.

To our surprise when he pulled up the boards, we found a beautiful antique mantel clock nestled between the floor joists! After the discovery of the clock, there were never any objects left in the hallway again.

Graveyard Ghosts

These types of spirits are generally seen at or around a cemetery in the days or weeks immediately following their burial, but before they either cross over or return to a place they loved in life.

Some graveyard ghosts do not cross over in this manner and can appear by their grave years after they've passed. I personally have had this type of event happen to me.

I was researching a home and went to the local cemetery to have a look at the family plot to see who else was buried there and might be important to the history of this particular family.

My friend and I arrived in broad daylight, and when we were approaching the graves of the family a white mist formed above one of the graves and soon took the rough form of a young woman. She looked right at us and pointed to an empty space in the family plot before disappearing.

This got us curious, so we did a little research. In a transcript of an oral history we found at the library, we read about how this young woman's grandparents had once been buried at this cemetery but were disinterred and moved to another cemetery on the other side of the state. All this happened as a result of a court order granted to a daughter of this couple.

The young woman who appeared to us was still alive when her grandparents both died and must have been confused as to why they weren't buried where she remembered them. Our thought is that she was trying to tell us that something was missing and she was confused.

Upon learning of the fate of the bodies of this young woman's grandparents, we returned to the cemetery and stood over this young woman's grave and gently explained to her what had happened and why.

We never saw her again, and we can only hope that our filling in the blanks for her is now allowing her to rest in the peace she deserves.

Transitional Spirits

These types of spirits can appear to family members or close friends, and normally appear to people soon after the spirit has died. Their appearance may last a few moments and might only involve the dead person's voice calling out the name of the living person with whom the spirit is trying to communicate.

Most paranormal researchers consider these types of spirits as similar in nature to crisis apparitions, because once a message is conveyed or communication is established, they tend not to appear again.

Portals

Portals are a subject of great controversy in the world of paranormal researchers and scientists alike. The controversy stems from whether or not portals even exist.

Paranormal researchers believe that portals are like a gate that opens up in certain locations and allows spirits, both good and bad, to easily travel from one location to another. Some paranormal researchers also believe that these portals are openings from the spirit world to this world.

Many scientists believe it is impossible for a portal to exist, let alone for anything to travel through a portal at will. Of course, many of these scientists don't believe in ghosts, so obviously the notion of spirits traveling through a portal would seem foolish to them.

People who are strong proponents of portals believe that portals are not limited to one location, area, or any particular sacred ground, although they are most often spotted around graveyards or waterways.

Child Ghosts

Child ghosts really tug at my heartstrings, as most of them are simply lost and looking for their mothers. While Hollywood and writers alike have, at times, made child ghosts out to be villains, most child ghosts are simply the spirits of children who have died, and are quite sad, lonely, and scared.

In some cases when parents have lost a child, that child may appear to the parents as a ghost in order to reassure them.

In other cases, the parents who have suffered this type of tragic loss can't let go of the child, and the child is unable to cross over to the other side. This situation is sad, both for the parents and for the child. The child in this type of case is waiting for permission from his or her parents to go to the other side, and it's important that the parents tell the child it is okay to do this.

Cases exist in which child ghosts are perfectly happy residing in the home they haunt. One such case is that of a little girl who occupies her old house, which was built in the nineteenth century.

The people who live in this house adore her, and this little girl ghost is very fond of rolling balls across the floor, throwing the ball over the stair rail and watching it bounce in the foyer below, and quietly playing in the bedroom the homeowners have decorated for her in period furniture and toys.

This might sound a little extreme to many people, but it is one way a family has adapted to having a ghost in their house. They cohabitate very peacefully and enjoy having the little girl around. Of course they established boundaries as you would with any child, and this particular child ghost is very well behaved and polite, which would have been the custom when she was alive.

The owners of this house have done extensive research in an effort to determine the identity of this little girl, but they can find no record of a child dying in their home. They have come to the conclusion that perhaps her original home was torn down, and she simply moved in to their house because it probably was of the same era and she felt comfortable there.

Parasitic Entities

Parasitic entities are a form of spirit that attaches itself to living people and, in a leech-like manner, attempts to suck the life energy out of the person to whom it is connected. These types of entities come in many different forms. Another, more common phrase associated with parasitic energies is *spirit attachment.*

It is widely believed that some forms of these spirits are human and some are not. Either way, they are extremely dangerous.

Some of the most common symptoms associated with parasitic entities are lack of motivation, dizziness, weakness, unclear thoughts, addictions to certain drugs or activities, unusual and extreme fatigue, restless sleep, and extreme nightmares.

While you may be experiencing some of these symptoms, don't jump to the conclusion that you are being attacked by a parasitic entity. It could be a physical ailment, and you should consult your physician immediately to rule out any physiological or mental causes.

If a parasitic entity is allowed to continue to literally suck the life out of you, your body may not have the strength to fight off any illness.

Demons

Demons are by far the most wretched, vile creatures I've ever come across. I've only run into one while ghost hunting, and it's not an experience I'm ready to repeat anytime soon.

The truth is, I never really believed in the existence of demons. I felt they were an invention of the church and were used to keep followers in line. I couldn't have been more wrong.

I can now say without hesitation: demons do exist and can cause great physical and psychological harm to their intended victims and those around them.

In some cases, demons have been known to cause injuries to people, such as welts, scratches, bite marks, and the like. However, these entities mostly attack psychologically, causing overwhelming anxiety, fear, and other types of negative emotions. The more emotional upset that they can cause in the environment in which they are residing, the better for them.

The presence of such a spirit could be accompanied by a foul stench that often resembles sulfuric acid, rotten eggs, or decomposing flesh, as well as, in some cases, a low, menacing growl.

They can cause people to feel anger, hate, sadness, and evil. Demons in particular may cause the air to feel thick and the temperature to change drastically. They can also make verbal threats, throw objects, push, shove, hit, and scratch.

In my first encounter with this kind of ghost, I was walking up to the front of an old home and heard a low, throaty growl from behind the door. It sounded like a very large, very mean dog. The owners of the property were not living there at the time, and they did not own any animals. Only much later was I able to determine where the growl came from, and it was not from any living creature.

While demons are capable of physical violence, they generally prefer psychological warfare. They can target one individual or an entire family and put negative or "bad" thoughts into their heads, causing people to act out in ways they normally wouldn't.

The more stress, anxiety, and emotional and mental distress a demon can cause in a family, the stronger the demon becomes. Many paranormal researchers believe that demons and other negative entities feed off of the negative energy.

Some demons will try to isolate one member of a family to the point that the only thing that person can rely on is the demon. This is not about possession. This is about control.

If someone in a family starts to withdraw, exhibit behavior that is not normal for them, or verbally and/or physically attacks other family members, friends, strangers, and so forth, it's possible that a demon is silently at work in that household.

A family member who is behaving this way could also be under the influence of drugs or alcohol, or be experiencing some type of psychological disorder. This person should be evaluated by a medical professional and undergo blood work, a urinalysis, and other tests to rule out any medical cause for this behavior. Don't just assume that because a family member is acting in this manner that it is a demon. Rule out all other logical explanations first.

A demon can also be attracted to a person who is mentally ill, someone suffering from depression, or a household filled with people who are constantly fighting with each other or are under an unusual amount of stress.

In a demonic haunting it is not uncommon for the demon to pose as a friend, as a loved one, or as another human spirit in order to gain your trust.

Demons can't *make* you do anything, but they can try to convince you to do what they want you to do. They can put suggestions and thoughts into your mind.

Demons can also play mind games with you, and in some cases use physical intimidation in an effort to put you in an emotionally and psychologically weak state—which would make it easier for the demon to control you.

If you believe your home is being occupied by any type of demonic being, do not try to handle the situation on your own. You should immediately seek the assistance of a trusted member of clergy or a paranormal investigation team that has the knowledge and experience to deal with this type of being.

Demons are very cunning, and it is possible to get caught up in the elaborate web they weave with little effort. In fact, in my case, by the time I realized what was happening, it was almost too late.

Many of my friends were very interested in the investigation I was working on in the vacant house that the demon dwelled in. They would ask that I take them past the house or into the house. At first I would drive them by the house. Within a few days of me taking them by the house, however, either they or a member of their family would become ill or be involved in some kind of accident. Not serious enough to cause any permanent harm or illness, but serious enough that it would require a few visits to the doctor or a short stay in the hospital. This happened three or four times with different friends of mine, so I stopped taking people by the house.

Even after I stopped bringing friends by the house, they would still ask about the case when I spoke with them on

the telephone. In some instances, the phone would discon-
nect or a large amount of interference would occur during
our discussions.

After a while, friends with whom I talked on the phone
about this case, or one of their family members, would fall
ill or yet again be involved in some type of minor accident.
So I quit talking about the case to everyone for fear some
harm would befall them.

It was a period of months before I figured out that the
demon had totally isolated me from my friends and family
in that there was now no one I could talk to about the case
or the demon, because I was afraid someone was going to
get hurt.

This demon had exercised a very high form of psychological warfare and almost won. It had succeeded in using
basic human psychology to try to isolate me. It's human
nature to want to protect your family and friends from any
possible harm. Knowing this, the demon used this human
psychological trait to manipulate me. Very scary stuff.

Once I realized exactly what this demon had almost
succeeded in doing, I took it upon myself to learn everything I could about this type of inhuman entity.

Some people believe that demons can "mark" you, and
when they do, they are able to find you anytime and anywhere they want. I was one of the people who didn't believe that demons could do that.

I'd been away from that house for years after it was
torn down without any further incident or sign of the

demon that once lived there. Then one day, quite recently in fact, I went to the grocery store. On the way home the rain started to fall rather heavily, but I had to stop for gas.

You know that canopy at gas stations that covers the pump area to protect you from inclement weather? I pulled up to the pump, but the front of my truck stuck out from the canopy. After pumping my gas, I got back into my truck and looked out the windshield. There, written in the raindrops across the glass, was the name of the demon that had lived in that house.

I was stunned. I knew there had been no one around my vehicle, and if there had been the odds of them knowing the name of that demon were about a zillion to one.

Some paranormal researchers and people of certain religions believe you should never speak the name of a demon because they feel it summons the demon.

I believe the opposite. I think that knowing the name of your enemy, especially a demon, gives you some type of power over the demon. This is why: several types of entities, demons among them, can appear to be something or someone other than what they really are in order to make you feel comfortable.

Calling out the demon's name keeps the demon honest, for lack of a better phrasing. It tells the demon that you are not fooled by its trickery, and are aware of exactly who or what it is. Sometimes this and this alone is enough to give you a small measure of control over the demon and the situation. It also can make you feel a bit empowered that you were able to see through its ruse.

Now, I'm not saying to go around calling out a demon's name and calling every spirit a demon. That would be foolish. You have to remember that encountering a demon is extremely rare, and the only reason I encountered one in my life is because I actively ghost hunt, and because of that the odds were greatly increased that sooner or later I would cross paths with one of these vile creatures. Most people will probably never encounter one of these horrible creatures in their lifetime.

Incubus and Succubus

These two types of spirits fall under the demon/inhuman category. An incubus is a type of male demon whose only desire is to have sex with a living woman. Its counterpart, a succubus, is a female demon who will attack a man in order to have sexual intercourse with him.

Their origins are steeped in myth and folklore that date back hundreds if not thousands of years. In some tales, incubi and succubi were demons who were able to change their gender in order to take the semen from a man as a succubus and then be able to transform into an incubus in order to impregnate a woman.

Some stories from folklore indicate that an incubus and/or succubus can shapeshift and resemble someone the person it wants to attack knows and is comfortable with. There are other tales that say these types of beings may visit the same person more than once.

Some religions believe that a succubus or incubus can cause a living person's health to become poor, or in some cases even cause death due to repeated visitations.

In many countries throughout Europe, it was widely believed that the children of an incubus or succubus caused witches, demons, and mentally or physically deformed or handicapped people to be born.

One of the first written stories of an incubus comes out of Mesopotamia. In Greece, an incubus was thought to be a type of priest who would visit people while they slept, bringing prophetic dreams. It was widely believed that this priest would plant the prophecy in someone's head while he or she slept and let it incubate over night.

The concept of "incubation" was carried over into early Christianity, where it became known as "keeping watch" or sitting a vigil. Early Christian churches encouraged their members who were experiencing problems or some type of difficulty to stay in the church all night in order to receive a vision that would guide them in the right direction. As time went on, however, the incubus and succubus were turned into demons and no longer thought of as a guardian or protector, and the practice was then discouraged.

Medieval society was obsessed with the sexual sins of women—so much so that women who were pregnant and not married would blame an incubus when in need of an excuse to hide an extramarital relationship. The people's belief in incubi was so real that rapists were known to blame an incubus to prevent being punished for raping a woman in her sleep.

Also during the Middle Ages, many women and priests explained rapes of women as a paranormal event instead of admitting that the women were raped by someone they held in a position of trust.

While there are still reports of people being attacked by an incubus or succubus, it is often hard to separate whether these people were attacked or whether they were suffering from sleep paralysis.

Sleep paralysis generally happens during the REM state of sleep, when the body releases certain hormones that paralyze it in order to prevent it from acting out during dreams, thus reducing the likelihood of physical harm during sleep.

Most of the time these hormones wear off before we wake up, but in some cases they don't, and people may wake up and feel temporarily paralyzed. When this occurs, it can feel like there's an evil presence in the room.

It is sometimes difficult to discern whether someone has been attacked by an incubus or succubus or whether it is an issue with sleep paralysis.

In many recent cases it could be either option. Without having spoken to any of the people who post in different paranormal forums to determine whether they have been attacked by an incubus or succubus, or whether they experienced an episode of sleep paralysis, it would be unfair for me to present these cases here.

People who have experienced such an attack will swear they were being attacked by some type of demon, and often doctors and other medical personnel are too quick to write off such an attack as sleep paralysis.

There is much debate in both the medical and the paranormal worlds about whether incubi or succubi even exist. Do they really exist? I can't say for sure. I've never personally run across one, but I am keeping an open mind.

Elementals

The category of elementals can cover a broad range of possible types of spirits and can cause what many perceive to be hauntings.

Elementals are thought to be nature spirits, and the belief in elementals in Ireland, Scotland, and other parts of Europe is quite common. Creatures such as gremlins, leprechauns, pixies, or fairies would fall under this category. While these creatures are generally thought to be a part of myth and legend, to many people they are very real.

In certain religions, elementals are believed to be the spirits that rule nature. They are called elementals because they correspond to the elements of earth, air, fire, and water, which each have various characteristics.

People have believed in elementals since before the beginning of any formal religion. Belief in elementals at one time was very commonplace. However, most Christian churches convinced their followers that elementals didn't exist because they couldn't be seen.

Gnomes, or earth elementals, were thought to live underground, under rocks and trees. They were believed to help those who respected nature.

The sylphs, or air elementals, were said to live on mountaintops and help humans with inspiration.

Water elementals, or undines, were said to closely resemble humans—unless the undines lived in ponds, rivers, waterfalls, and the like. People believed that water elementals were very friendly toward humans.

Fire elementals, called salamanders, were believed to help keep humans warm. Some cultures held that without fire elementals, humanity would have never discovered fire.

It is widely believed that elementals are born from chaos magic such as Voodoo, HooDoo, and other forms of magic. It is also widely accepted among paranormal researchers that elementals have to be summoned in some manner and will very rarely haunt a location without being invited to do so.

As far as I know, there is only one documented case of an elemental and that case is in Ireland. Leap Castle is reported to be one of the most haunted places in Ireland. The castle was built around 800 CE by the O'Bannon family, who were the secondary chieftains in the area subject to the ruling of the powerful and warmongering O'Carrolls.

In the sixteenth century, the bloodshed between the different clans in Ireland reached a climax, and it would not be unusual for people to be invited to dinner at the castle and then brutally murdered.

The Bloody Chapel, so named because Teige O'Carroll murdered his brother at the altar, is where the elemental is most often seen. This elemental is described as a vile, hunched creature that is always accompanied by a smell, such as sulfur or a rotting dead body.

There's a story that a woman who lived in the castle summoned an elemental to do her bidding and that this elemental still resides there, carrying out its assigned duties.

Some paranormal researchers believe that elementals are summoned to carry out specific duties, and they will continue to perform the tasks asked of them until they are sent away.

Some people believe that all elementals are negative entities, but personally I don't agree. I think they could be protecting something or someone and will go to extremes to do so. Does this make them bad? I guess it would depend on your point of view.

Angelic Beings

Throughout history, and into the modern era, people have reported encounters with angels. The circumstances involving angel encounters seem to center around an angel or angels coming to a person in times of tragedy or great emotional strife in order to provide comfort and, in some cases, assistance to the person in need. Many times angels are viewed as messengers.

People report seeing angels in different forms, but in the majority of angel encounters the angels appear in a human form. It has also been reported that when an angel appears, it is accompanied by an increased sense of colors, particularly greens and blues. Angels have also been known to be associated with certain scents, such as roses, pine, or sandalwood.

According to those who study angel appearances, an angel could appear as a child, a relative who has passed away, a neighbor, friend, or a winged being.

Also under the category of angelic beings are *guardian angels*. Many people believe that an angel is assigned to you at birth to watch over you and gently guide and protect you during your lifetime. According to this line of thought, a guardian angel could be a person from your family who passed away before you were born, or an enlightened soul who is given the duty to be your guardian throughout your life.

Sometimes angels don't appear as a being at all, but just as light. Or someone encountering an angel may be overcome with a feeling of unconditional love, comfort, and contentment.

Spirit Guides

Spirit guides are beings that are assigned to us by God, the Goddess, or whatever higher power you believe in, before we're born to assist us throughout our lives. Some guides remain with you throughout your entire life, while other guides will come and go as you face certain situations in your life.

Spiritualists and many New Age thinkers believe that spirit guides have different levels of consciousness themselves. They could be ascended masters, or normal spirits that may excel in a certain area.

Spirit guides can help us in many ways. They can give us certain signs to get us to pay attention to something we need to know. Signs can be a string of seeming coincidences that just can't be ignored. Pay attention to these little things when you notice them. It means there's a message there.

You know that feeling you get in your gut when you're facing a decision, or when you're in some other difficult situation? Chances are that is one of your guides nudging you in the direction you should go. I know personally that when I ignore that gut feeling, things don't turn out well; but when I listen to that feeling in my gut, things tend to turn out fine.

Guides can also give you intuitive insight, and most of the time you won't even know where it came from. For example, have you at different times heard a voice in your head telling you to do something? That could be one of your guides.

One example: I was vacationing in northern Michigan one year and walking through some short grass on the way to a beach. I was lost in the beautiful scenery and not really paying too much attention to where I was walking. Suddenly a voice popped into my head: "Stop!"

I stopped and looked around and saw a huge rattle-snake curled up about six feet in front of me. Had I not heard that voice and paid attention to it, I would have walked directly up on it and not even realized it. Was it one of my guides that warned me to stop or just a coincidence? I don't really believe in coincidences, so the answer is obvious.

Guardians

In some religions, people believe in entities called guardians or watchers. These are not to be confused with guardian angels or the angels who were sent by God in the Bible, also called watchers.

This type of guardian or watcher is a special form of entity that followers of these belief systems believe are sent to watch over and protect women when they reach a mature age, usually sometime in their mid-to-late fifties.

It's very rare to actually see a watcher, but women who have seen them report them to be robed with hoods over their heads, hiding their faces. I know they sound scary, but in reality they are very kind to their charges. They have been known to go to great lengths if the need arises in order to protect the woman they were sent to take care of.

Watchers are not there to interfere with a woman's life, but rather to help and guide her through the last stages of her life.

Conclusion

There are many types of paranormal events and different types of spirits. Every spirit will be a little different and generally have its own motivation for acting the way it does.

Imagine for a moment that you have died but you don't know you are dead. You return to your home and carry on all the activities you normally do, except someone else is living in your home and all your possessions are gone.

How would you feel? Confused? Angry? Sad? Frustrated? Or all of these things? That is how some spirits feel. They can't talk to anyone; no one can see them; and they act out to get attention, acknowledgement, or help.

The truth is that just because a ghost may be acting out doesn't necessarily make it a negative spirit. Ghosts are just trying by any means they can to get someone's attention. Try talking to the spirit instead of being afraid of it. Tell the ghost that you know it is there and that you acknowledge its presence.

You may be wondering why I included such beings as guardians and angels in this chapter along with other types of ghosts. It's because they are all forms of entities that may or may not be in your home.

You do not have to be afraid of beings such as guardians, angels, and spirit guides. More than likely, you will not even be aware these types of entities are around you at all. Just keep in mind that they do exist, and while their behavior typically will not account for most types of paranormal activity taking place in your home, there are times when an angel, guardian, and/or spirit guide may be trying to get your attention by behaving in ways that are not normally associated with these types of spirits.

Using your notes and entries from your journal (see chapter 6), perhaps you've been able to figure out what type of spirit is inhabiting your home. Additionally, you may have been able to determine whether the ghost or spirit is a good spirit or some type of negative spirit that is out to cause harm.

If you've come to the conclusion that the ghost or spirit is a family member or other loved one who has died, most of your fear should be gone, because you know who it is. In fact, I'd say that if this is the case, you've been able to find some comfort in the fact that your loved one is still trying to maintain some form of relationship with you and your family.

On the other hand, if you're afraid that the ghost or spirit is a negative type of entity, you may be more scared than ever. Don't be. Being afraid may only make the negative ghost or spirit more powerful. You should consult either a trusted religious figure or a reputable paranormal investigation team to help you with this problem.

CHAPTER 5

How to Talk to
Your Children About Ghosts

If your children are very small, you won't want to tell them everything, of course, but do encourage them to share their stories with you. This not only builds trust between you and your child, but also gives the child an opportunity to talk to you about other things that may be going on in his or her life.

If your child is experiencing nightmares, ask what he or she dreamed about and pay close attention to the response. The nightmare may not be a dream at all, but a way of telling you what happened.

While many children have imaginary friends, in a home with paranormal activity that friend may not be so imaginary at all. If your child has an imaginary friend, ask questions about the friend in a gentle manner so as to not alarm your child.

In particular, take note if your child's imaginary friend is telling your child to do something your child knows is wrong, or something you know your son or daughter is incapable of coming up with independently.

If your child comes to you and says, "I saw a ghost," you may not know how to handle this situation in a way that will not frighten your child. This chapter will explain the *do*s and *don't*s of talking to children about ghosts.

The Dos

Gently talk to your child about what he or she experienced, saw, or heard. By taking the time to get the whole story, you won't jump to any conclusions and you will have all the facts as your child perceived them. Having this knowledge will help you understand what your child experienced and will give you a better idea of how to handle the situation. It will also help you to figure out if your child really encountered a spirit, or if your son or daughter just has an imaginary friend.

While your child is telling you about the experience, give your full attention. This will make your son or daughter feel more comfortable as well as convey that what you are hearing is important. It will also encourage your child to tell you the entire story and not just parts of it. Sometimes if children don't think they have our attention, or feel we are distracted and not really paying attention to what they are saying, they will not tell us everything that happened.

If your child seems to be upset or afraid, take the time to snuggle up together in a chair or on the sofa. Wait for your child to calm down and feel safe and comfortable, and then ask that he or she tell you what caused the upset or fear. The odds are that your child thinks that ghosts are bad and is worried about getting hurt in some way. Once you take away this fear, your son or daughter will be more likely to open up to you and share what happened.

As a parent, your child looks to you for protection. Make sure you tell your children that you will help them understand their experience and that they are not alone. Always be sure to thank them for telling you what happened, and assure them that you will do everything you can to make this problem go away so they won't be scared or upset anymore.

Ask how the experience made your child feel. It's vitally important to get an idea about how your son or daughter feels about this new friend. Children may tell you that they are happy to have someone new to play with, but make sure you keep an eye on the situation and ask them every couple of days how they feel about their new playmate. If you notice that your child is becoming stressed out, afraid, or nervous, or starting to withdraw from family and friends, immediately talk to him or her and try to figure out what the new friend did or is doing to provoke this behavioral change.

To monitor the situation between your child and this new friend, ask to be told what your child and the friend do together. What kind of games do they play? What do they talk about? Don't pressure your child; instead, use gentle but probing questions to try to figure out if your son or daughter's friend has been asking or telling him or her to do certain things that your child knows are wrong, or if your child's friend has been telling your kid things that you know aren't true.

Be on the lookout for any shifts in the behavior of your child. If children begin to act in ways they normally wouldn't or become withdrawn and moody, you should immediately have a talk with them to find out what their friend has been doing to them or telling them.

The Don'ts

You don't want to confuse children by telling them that ghosts don't exist or that they made up the whole story. If your child really did have a paranormal experience and yet you say that ghosts don't exist, it could be very confusing. Moreover, your kids might not tell you about any other paranormal experiences they have because they feel you don't believe them.

Our children mimic our behavior. If you become upset, frustrated, or hysterical because of what your children tell you, you could scare them tremendously and put them under an undue amount of unnecessary stress. As a parent, you need to remain calm and really listen to what your child is telling you about any experience.

If your children are older, do not encourage them to use a Ouija board, hold a séance, or engage in any other activity that could cause more problems. Most of the time a Ouija board and/or séance will only make matters worse.

Behind the Ouija board is the theory that its users are opening a door or portal to the other side. Anything, good or evil, can come through that open door, and there is no way to stop it or control it. The same is true with séances. A séance can get out of control very easily, because it is impossible for an inexperienced medium to control what or who comes through that open doorway.

In many cases, it takes a lot of courage for children, especially older children, to confide in their parents. When they are telling you about their experience, remain objective and don't express any doubt about how they perceived the events they are describing. Don't tell them that they just have an overactive imagination or otherwise dismiss what they are telling you. If your kids think that you don't believe them, you have shut the door of communication, and they may not tell you about something worse that happens to them later on.

If you decide to share what your child told you with family members, friends, or co-workers, you will probably get a ton of advice on how to handle the situation. While these people mean well and are only trying to help, follow your instincts and only do what you feel comfortable with.

There is a ton of information on the Internet about ghosts and hauntings, and not all of it is accurate. If you are uncomfortable about what exactly to do when your child comes to you saying he or she has seen a ghost, you can contact me or you can contact a legitimate paranormal researcher in the area where you live. Don't be afraid to ask for help in dealing with this situation.

Many paranormal researchers believe that children from a very young age through their early teenage years are more likely to experience some type of paranormal phenomenon because they haven't developed the prejudices that many adults have against such things as ghosts.

They also haven't created their own way of filtering feelings and experiences that society may consider abnormal, irrational, or illogical.

Some researchers believe that it could just be that children's brains are physically more receptive to paranormal experiences, because they are young and their brains are still developing.

Children seem to have encounters with the paranormal more often than adults do. Paranormal researchers generally believe that this is due to the fact that children haven't become as jaded and as programmed by society as adults, and that they are more open to the paranormal. For these reasons it is so important that your children feel that they can come and talk to you about what they are experiencing.

Are You Raising a Psychic Child?

Having been born a psychic child, I can fully understand and appreciate the difficulties associated with being gifted. I say *gifted* because the word *psychic* really bothers me for a multitude of reasons—and the number one reason involves the negative connotations associated with the word due to the great number of frauds who call themselves psychic and take advantage of people in desperate need of help.

I believe the abilities that I and so many others have been given are gifts from a higher power. You can call that higher power God, Allah, Buddha, whatever.

Imagine being a four-year-old child and being able to see ghosts everywhere and interact with them. Imagine telling your parents as much, only to have them take you to psychiatrist after psychiatrist to find out what is "wrong" with you—and then almost institutionalizing you because they didn't understand what was really happening.

Now imagine that this gifted child, after almost being institutionalized, is no longer able to tell her parents about the ghosts and beings that she sees just about everywhere. Having to keep it all a secret and bottling it up inside— learning at a young age that she can trust no one with the knowledge that she can see and communicate with ghosts.

Imagine how alone and isolated that child feels. That was me. Don't let that happen to your gifted child.

It is possible that some of the paranormal activity occurring in your home could be due to the fact that your child is gifted with abilities that draw ghosts to him or her and the rest of your family. That's why I thought it so important to talk about gifted children in this book.

Think of it this way: you know how when it's really dark outside, and you turn on an outside light and every bug in three counties swarms around that light? In the spirit world, a child or adult who is gifted with the ability to see and/or communicate with spirits is that light, and spirits will swarm around that person the same way a bug does to a light in pitch darkness.

A child who is gifted should be treated like any other child who may be gifted. Whether children are gifted academically, musically, artistically, or with psychic gifts, they need to be able to have their abilities nurtured and learn to adjust to and appreciate their gifts. This will empower them to achieve whatever their goals are in the future.

If your child tells you he has seen angels, relatives who have passed, or other types of apparitions, and you react negatively to this information, your child will think he is "bad" or has done something wrong. As a parent, your children look up to you and want your guidance, understanding, and, most of all, your acceptance of their abilities.

Remember: gifted children are very sensitive and need love, compassion, and care. I've listed below and on the following pages some tips to raising a gifted child.

Be Alert

Keep track of any changes in your child's behavior, such as symptoms of depression, sleeping problems, isolation, and moodiness. You may wake up in the morning and find your child sleeping in your bed or on the floor of your bedroom. Be sure and talk to your child at the first opportunity to find out the reasons for going into your room during the night.

It's not unusual for children who are being visited by spirits in the middle of the night to flee to their parents' bedroom, or to be scared to tell their parents about what they are experiencing. Many children feel that what they are experiencing is their fault, and they may be afraid to tell you about their experiences because they feel they've done something wrong or bad. They may also believe that you will tell them what they experienced was only a bad dream or their imagination.

One of the worst things for a child who is being visited by ghosts is to not have her parents believe her, or to have his parents think he is lying or making it up to get attention.

If your child doesn't think you believe what he or she is telling you is happening, this could cause your child to feel isolated and alone. If children develop those feelings, it could make them easy prey for different types of negative ghosts or entities that will use those feelings to try and control them.

Read and Learn

Take the time to study the paranormal. You and your child could benefit from learning how other gifted people deal with their unique abilities. You may want to visit your local bookstore or shop online for an excellent book about dream symbolism. This type of book could become very helpful if your child is having vivid and sometimes scary dreams.

As a parent, you should arm yourself with knowledge so that you are able to answer in an honest, calm, and straightforward manner any questions your child may have.

By taking the time to educate yourself about the world of the paranormal and any psychic gifts your child may possess, you are not only empowering yourself but you're empowering your child as well.

Listen to Your Child

Really listen when your child wants to tell you about a particular dream or experience. Stop what you're doing and give your son or daughter your full attention. Listen carefully to what your child has to say, and ask questions about the dream or experience. Make sure you word your questions in such a way that they do not upset or scare your child any more than your child might be scared already.

The goal is to make him or her feel safe and secure, knowing that you are there to help understand the dream or experience.

Teach

Work with your children to help them become well-balanced. Children, especially gifted children, need to maintain a healthy diet, get a good amount of sleep every night, and spend time just being a kid. This should include playing with children their own age and participating in other activities like sports, after-school events, and any hobby or activity they particularly enjoy.

Pay Attention

Some children like the attention they get from their parents and other people if they've experienced paranormal activity, had nightmares, or claimed a ghost keeps waking them up at night. If your child is inventing these events to get attention, then by paying attention to your child and doing things with her that don't involve these dreams or experiences, the inventions will soon stop—because your kid will be getting the attention he craves in other ways.

If your child is truly experiencing paranormal activity, a paranormal researcher may be able to help you get rid of any ghosts, but once the ghost is gone, your child may, although unwittingly, invite it back because he or she misses the attention received when the ghost was there.

It's important that you explain to your child that inviting anything like a ghost into your home is not appropriate under any circumstances. A child's mind and soul are open to so many things that something negative or bad could be invited in by your child unintentionally.

The last thing you want is a negative entity of any type to enter your home and take up residence.

Conclusion

Children are by nature very open to the paranormal. They are also extremely prone to becoming easily startled or scared. Yet it's important that you share what is happening in your home with them. Your kids might be experiencing the same type of activity as you are, but for some reason are keeping it to themselves.

Children sometimes think that events in life are their fault, even though they clearly aren't, and they may not want to tell you about any paranormal experiences because they think they did something "bad."

By opening up the lines of communication with your children, you are enabling them to share any experiences they may have had without fear of judgment or ridicule.

If you're raising a psychic child, it's possible that he or she is living in constant terror of any ghosts or spirits that might be visiting your home on a consistent basis.

Psychic children realize at a very young age that they are "different" from other kids and adults. This can be awkward and uncomfortable for a psychic child whose only goal is to be "normal" and fit in.

Give psychic children permission to be themselves without the constant fear of being criticized or judged. Keep in mind that many psychic children hide their gifts from their friends because they don't want to be teased or be ostracized from their peer group.

Having been a psychic child myself, I found out early that when you tell your friends and others that you can see dead people, you quickly become an outsider and are often ignored. This can lead to low self-esteem and feelings of isolation.

You do not want your child to feel this way, since there are certain negative entities that can prey on your child while he or she is in this state. The most important thing you can do as a parent of a psychic child is to accept your child and his or her gifts and do everything in your power to give your son or daughter a sense of belonging and normalcy.

CHAPTER 6

Gathering Proof

The more evidence you can pull together, the easier it is to find any patterns to the type of paranormal activity you're experiencing. This evidence will also be of great assistance to a paranormal researcher if you decide you need to call one into your home.

In this chapter I'll explain what evidence you can collect and how to do it.

Journal

It's important to keep a journal or some type of record of any possible paranormal activity. The journal should include:

Time and Date

Note the time and date of any possible paranormal activity. You will also want to try to write down how long the event lasted.

For example, a possible notation may look like this: *06/23/11, 10:32 a.m. I heard footsteps in the hallway by the bedrooms. Home alone at the time. The footsteps lasted about 1 minute.*

Who Saw the Event?

You will want to write down who witnessed the paranormal event and what mood they were in at the time of the activity.

So our example above will change to: *06/23/11, 10:32 a.m. I heard footsteps in the hallway by the bedrooms. Home alone at the time. The footsteps lasted about 1 minute.*

My mood at the time: most excellent.

Has This Happened Before?

Include in your journal notes whether this same person or people have witnessed the same activity before.

This will change our example to: *06/23/11, 10:32 a.m. I heard footsteps in the hallway by the bedrooms. Home alone at the time. The footsteps lasted about 1 minute.*

My mood at the time: most excellent. Have heard the footsteps before.

The Circumstances

If what you experienced was visual, you'll want to make a notation of what the lighting was like at the time—for example: *dark, moonlit, sunlight,* or *daylight*—and if you heard any sounds at the same time you saw the event occurring. Make a note about anything else that was happening at the time: for example, *phone rang, television on, radio on,* and so forth.

So our example could change to something like: *06/23/11, 10:32 a.m. I heard footsteps in the hallway by the bedrooms. Home alone at the time. The footsteps lasted about 1 minute.*

My mood at the time: most excellent. Have heard the footsteps before. All radios and televisions were off at the time.

Because footsteps are not visual, there is no need to note the kind of lighting present during the event used in our example.

Other People in the Home

If anyone else was home during the paranormal event, make a notation about who was home, where they were, and what they were doing at the time the paranormal event occurred.

Other Witnesses

If the paranormal activity was witnessed by other people, write down everyone who witnessed the activity. Make a note of their mental state, behavior, and the like.

Additional Information

Write down anything else you feel is relevant to the paranormal activity while it is still fresh in your mind. Take note of how you felt when the event occurred. Did the area get cold? Hot? Did you feel threatened, or were you just startled or scared? Did you smell anything unusual at the time the event occurred?

If other people witnessed the event, have them write down in their own words what they experienced and how they felt during the event.

Tell Your Family

Other members of your family who live with you will often keep paranormal activity they've experienced to themselves. This is especially true with teenagers and small children.

By being open and honest with the other people living in your home, you open up a line of discussion in which other family members will feel more comfortable sharing any experiences they've had.

Tell your family that you're keeping a journal of the events that are happening in your home. Encourage them either to write down their experiences in the journal or to tell you about them right after they occur so you can write them down together.

I understand that you may be hesitant to open up this line of discussion with members of your family, because you don't want to scare or alarm them. Chances are, however, that if you're experiencing paranormal activity, so are they.

When you do talk to your family about the paranormal experiences you've been having, do it when you're calm and not upset by an event that just occurred. This is more important if you have children living at home.

Children will take their cues from you. If you're upset and overly emotional, that will transfer to your children and could cause them unnecessary stress and worry. If you remain calm, they will remain calm.

In addition, if your family comes together as a united front against the ghosts or spirits occupying your home, it will make you stronger than if you try to handle the situation by yourself.

Many types of ghosts or spirits thrive off dividing a family unit and causing chaos and disharmony. If your entire family supports one another, this empowers you and puts these types of spirits at a great disadvantage.

One way to do this to keep the lines of communication open. When you or a family member witnesses a possible paranormal event, try to debunk it right away with your family's help.

For example, if your son was walking down a hallway and a door slammed shut, go with him to the hallway and ask him to describe to you exactly what happened, where he was standing or walking, and so forth.

Try to duplicate the activity. If a door slammed shut, open it and look for an open window or a ceiling fan left on. Leave the door open and have your son walk down the hall again, and see if his footsteps might be causing the door to vibrate enough to close on its own.

Check the door itself to see if it will swing shut without much effort. It could be that some type of vacuum was created by another door opening or closing when the person left another room to make the door in question slam shut.

If you can't duplicate the activity, have the person who witnessed it write about it in the journal, or you can do it for the person.

Look for a Pattern

Once you have a few journal entries, check to see if a pattern of possible paranormal activity is emerging. Is the activity always around one particular person in the home? Does the activity happen at the same time every day, or on a particular day? Is the activity different every time, or is the same activity repeating itself in the same place at the same time, every time?

If the pattern of activity is occurring at the same time all the time and never alters its schedule, and the activity is always the same—for example, if footsteps are heard every morning at six a.m.—then chances are it's a residual haunting. (See chapter 3 for more information on residual hauntings.)

However, if the activity is happening at different times and is not always the same, it could be a traditional or intelligent haunting (also see chapter 3). As an example, if you see an apparition and it acknowledges you or interacts with you in some way, then you know you're dealing with an intelligent ghost or spirit.

Conclusion

Remember: paranormal activity does not mean your house is haunted. By keeping a journal, it will be easier for you and/or a paranormal researcher to determine:

1) if there is a pattern to the activity;

2) what type of spirit, if any, is present in your home; and

3) whether you are just experiencing some paranormal events, or whether your house has a residual, traditional, or inhuman haunting.

CHAPTER 7

Research the Past

It is not unusual for the previous owners of a property to haunt their old home. It's also possible for a piece of land to be haunted, not the dwelling itself.

By researching your property, you can, in some instances, determine the identity of the spirit haunting your home. If you live in the United States, the first place to start is usually at the courthouse in the county in which you live.

There are many different kinds of records stored at the courthouse in your county seat. It's important to start with the basics and work your way through the rest of them. Also note that you may not even need to go to the courthouse: much of this information is now online as well. Check your county's website to see what is available there, and call a county or local government employee for help if you need it.

Land Records

If you do go to the courthouse, you will want to check out the Register of Deeds. This department will have deeds, mortgages, and sometimes abstracts of your property.

You'll want to bring with you the property ID number located on your property-tax bill. If you don't have a property-tax statement handy, you can call the local government office that oversees property tax for your city and they will give you the number.

This research may take a little bit of time depending on how computerized your courthouse is, but it's worth the effort. The purpose of finding out the history of your land is to try to determine if the ghost in your home is that of a past owner of the land or of your home.

Once you have the names of any previous owners of your home and/or property, it's time to go to the Department of Vital Statistics (or a similar department) in the courthouse.

Death Records

Death records can contain some very good information and give you new places to search for information. Just keep in mind that some of the information on a death certificate was provided by a family member and may not always be very accurate—but for your purposes, all the information you need should be there.

Normally a death certificate will contain such information as place of birth and death, parents' names and places of birth, the name of the person who supplied the information for the death certificate, the cause of death, the name of the attending doctor, and the place of burial. The older the death, the less information the death certificate is likely to have.

With a death certificate, all you really are looking for is the date of death, the cause of death, and where the person died. Make a note of where the person is buried if the death certificate contains that information.

The reason for doing this research is so that you or a paranormal investigator can address any possible past owner by name. Addressing a ghost by its name can, in some cases, make it easier to get the ghost to move out of your house and to go where it belongs.

Historical Societies

If your town or county has a historical society, the employees there may also be able to provide you with some information on your property and the surrounding area.

Ask them if they have plat maps, which may show not only your piece of property but also the surrounding area at certain times in history. The Register of Deeds should also have this information. Get copies of all the information. You never know what might turn out to be important.

This information can prove to be invaluable when you're trying to figure out who may be haunting your home or is at the root of the paranormal activity you are experiencing.

Talk to the Neighbors

Of course I'm not telling you to tell your neighbors that you think your home may be haunted, but do ask relevant neighbors about the people who used to live in your home.

Make it a point to talk to the older residents of your neighborhood. Most of them have probably lived there for a great length of time and could have the piece of information you need.

By all means if they ask you point-blank if you have ghosts or if your house is haunted, be honest. I've found that people who ask that question normally have a very good reason for inquiring, and they may have stories about previous residents who have lived in your house who have experienced the same thing.

If this is the case, try to get those residents' names, addresses, and/or telephone numbers, and don't hesitate to make contact with them. You can tell them that you live in the house they once occupied and ask them if they experienced any weird incidents when they lived in your home.

The bottom line is that you need to set aside any worries about whether the previous owners will think you're strange. If your family is being scared or feeling threatened by the paranormal activity going on in your home, you must take any steps necessary to get to the bottom of it and come up with a plan of action.

Conclusion

This type of research is not for everyone, and it is totally understandable if you don't want to take the time to do it. A good paranormal investigator or ghost-hunting team should be able to complete this research for you.

However, I highly recommend doing the research yourself if at all possible. It will give you back some feeling of control of the situation, and it means you're taking a proactive rather than reactive stance when dealing with a ghost in your home.

CHAPTER 8

Answers to Frequently Asked Questions About the Paranormal

As a paranormal researcher, I've seen some unexplainable things and talked to hundreds if not thousands of people about the paranormal. People have lots of questions about ghosts and their behavior and motivations and about the paranormal in general.

So instead of sprinkling this information throughout the book, I thought it would be more beneficial to you, the reader, if the most common questions about ghosts and the paranormal were all contained in one chapter. So . . . here we go.

Frequently Asked Questions

Is there a difference between a ghost and a spirit?

Some people believe that ghosts are earthbound souls, and spirits are people who have died, crossed over, and chosen to come back for whatever reason.

In other words, proponents of this theory believe that earthbound souls can't, or won't, move on to the other side until they've delivered a message or fulfilled some purpose, or that they are otherwise not ready to leave the earthly plain. Earthbound souls could also not even realize they are dead.

Ghosts can be earthbound for any number of reasons. A person who died in her sleep might literally wake up dead. As funny as this may sound, such people honestly wouldn't have any recollection of dying or be aware of their death. They could go for years carrying out their day-to-day routine as they had in life. Imagine their frustration at wanting to communicate with people around them and not being able to do so, or having strangers move into their home that they still believe to be theirs.

Another, more complicated reason ghosts might remain earthbound is to avenge their death. In some cases a ghost might choose to remain here to ensure secrets guarded in life remain secrets and are not brought to the surface.

Spirits, on the other hand, know they're dead, have made the transition to the other side, but make a choice to return to their familiar surroundings on earth from time to time. Whether it's to check on the safety and welfare of loved ones, attend a special family function, or to communicate a message, they are not bound to do these things but rather it's their option to do them.

Can ghosts attach themselves to people?

The short answer is yes. The long answer is a tad more complicated. Ghosts have been known to attach themselves to certain people, but for very different reasons.

It could be that a loved one who has passed away will hang around you and follow you wherever you live. The ghost of a loved one is, of course, harmless but may act out in various ways to get your attention and let you know he or she is there.

For example, the ghost of a family member could cause a picture of himself or someone else in the family to fly off a wall or table. Such ghosts might move or do other things that in some way will tell you who they are, if you're paying attention.

Other types of ghosts who are not family members who have passed can also attach to a person. This type of ghost may or may not be friendly and could have ulterior motives.

No one really knows how a ghost that is not a family member who has passed determines who they want to attach to, but it's theorized that they choose someone who is weak, emotionally stressed, or depressed.

Some paranormal researchers believe that ghosts that are not related to the person they attach themselves to may be some form of demon, or another negative type of entity that wants to cause harm and upheaval in a family or just in one particular person's life.

The lesson here is that if you are experiencing some type of paranormal activity, look at it from a different perspective. Pay attention to the actions it takes, and see if you can figure out if it is a message from a departed loved one before assuming it is something bad or evil.

Are there certain types of people who could be affected by, or targeted by, a ghost or a demon for possession?

Ghosts may sometimes feel as though they are owed something from a person they perceived as having wronged them while they were alive. If a ghost feels it suffered some kind of injustice or unhappiness at the hands of a person who is still alive, this ghost may be seeking revenge.

Another possible reason is that the ghost has unfulfilled desires, wants, needs, and cravings that weren't fulfilled during its lifetime, and may find a person whose desires match its own closely. In this case, the ghost may try to possess that person to satisfy its needs.

A negative entity, such as a demon, might possess a person to stop the spread of spirituality. For example, if a person is practicing her religion very faithfully, the demon may want to stop the spread of spirituality both in the person and throughout the community. In order to achieve this aim, the demon might try to possess this person or drive her away from her religion.

A person with a prolonged physical illness may be a likely victim for an attack by a ghost or demon. Some people believe that a ghost or demon could target an injury or diseased area of a living person's body and use it as a point of entry.

People with a weak mind are easy targets for ghosts, demons, and negative entities in general. Living people who are filled with anger, greed, and/or are extremely emotional are prime candidates for an attack. Like a physical open wound, the negative spirit can enter this type of person's mind and take control. Once in, the negative spirit will use the person's own personality traits to control him or her with relative ease.

For example, if someone is highly emotional, the negative entity would make that person even more emotional—thus weakening the mind even further in order to continue to control that person for many months or years.

The bottom line is this: if you are spiritually stronger than the negative entity trying to take you over, you will win. If you're not, the negative entity wins. If you are a spiritually strong person, and you ask whatever higher power you believe in for protection, your chances of being possessed or attacked by a negative entity will decrease substantially.

Are there different ways ghosts and spirits communicate with the living?

Yes. There are times when a ghost or spirit will go out of its way in an attempt to get our attention and communicate.

If the ghost or spirit in your home is a loved one who has passed, you may smell an odor that reminds you of your loved one. In other cases, a deceased family member or friend may give you a hug, touch your shoulder, appear in your dreams, or give you a gift that you recognize as being from him or her.

A ghost or spirit may turn lights on and off or show up in pictures, or you might hear the ghost or spirit make noise, see them as an apparition, or feel that you are not alone.

If I'm in a haunted location, can a ghost follow me home?

Personally, I think a ghost can follow someone home, although there will be people in the paranormal-research field who will probably disagree with me. In most cases, a ghost will not follow you home, but there have been cases that suggest it's possible.

I believe that if a spirit follows you home, it is probably just curious about who you are, or it wants to make contact for some reason—such as to give you a message or relay some other type of information.

That's not to say a negative spirit won't follow you home to cause havoc in your life—because it could, although it is very uncommon. Remember that negative ghosts or entities are attracted to negative energy, such as fear.

If you are a religious person, you may want to say a prayer of protection before leaving an allegedly haunted location. If you know the Saint Michael prayer, it would be a good one to use. If you don't, here it is:

> *Saint Michael the Archangel, defend us in battle;*
> *be our protection against the wickedness and snares of*
> *the devil. May God rebuke him we humbly pray; and*
> *do thou, O Prince of the heavenly host, by the power of*
> *God, thrust into hell Satan and all the evil spirits who*
> *prowl about the world seeking the ruin of souls. Amen.*

This is the short form of the Saint Michael prayer, composed by Pope Leo XIII in 1886.

What happens to a ghost if the house it lives in is torn down?

My experience has been that if the house of a ghost is torn down, the ghost will relocate to a home in the same area.

Here's an example: one of the houses I'd investigated was inhabited by a ghost I'll call "Roger." The house was very old and was finally condemned and torn down.

The people who owned homes around where this old home stood immediately started to experience paranormal activity in their own homes when Roger's house was torn down. Roger, not ready or willing to move on to the other side, simply took up residence in a neighboring house.

Another example is that of a ghost that lived in my great-aunt's house. The house he'd occupied in life was torn down to make way for a gas station, so he moved into the second floor of her house and settled in.

If a ghost is going to stay earthbound by choice, then in the majority of cases such a ghost wants to be in familiar surroundings. If the location it chooses is destroyed, the ghost will more often than not stay in the same familiar territory.

What about home renovations and paranormal activity?

A direct correlation between home renovations and paranormal activity appears to exist. Some people will experience the onset of paranormal activity if they start to renovate their homes—even if they've never experienced paranormal activity in that house before the renovations. There are several theories regarding renovation ghosts.

A ghost may become upset or angry due to the disturbance of their comfort zone, which could cause them to become more active. If you experience this, it could help to explain out loud to the ghost what exactly the renovations are and how long it will be until the renovations are completed. Reassure the spirit that the work will make things more comfortable, not only for you and your family but for the ghost as well.

Some ghosts that are otherwise quiet may become protective of the home and protest by increasing paranormal activity. Yet other spirits may be so appreciative of the care and attention going into the renovation that they show their excitement through an increase in paranormal events.

The energy of construction is sometimes all that is necessary to provide enough strength for a ghost to act out. With construction come dozens of people all emitting energy, which can act as a battery to recharge a spirit.

Most renovation ghosts can make progress on a renovation slow down at times. I've heard of cases in which a ghost was so upset about the work going on in what it perceived to be its home that the ghost has hidden tools, moved construction materials, and caused such a ruckus that several of the contractors working on the house have fled in fear and refused to enter the house ever again.

However, in the majority of cases, once all work has stopped the renovation ghost should settle back down over a period of several weeks.

The most important thing with a renovation ghost is to be patient and just wait out the ghost's behavior.

Can brand-new homes be haunted?

Simply put: yes. If another home or another type of building was on the property in the past, it's possible that a ghost stayed tied to the land and will occupy any home or other structure built on that property.

For example, assume an older home was torn down to make room for your new home. The ghost might temporarily move into a neighboring house until your new home is built on the land where the first house originally stood. It's highly possible that the ghost could move into your new house because it was built on the land the old house occupied.

Your response might be that the land was always a field and never held another type of structure. This is well and good, but there is no way of knowing for sure that this field wasn't once the site of some type of encampment or the site of a tragic accident or some type of battle between Native American tribes or other people.

In short, a spirit will not attach itself to a piece of land without a good reason, even if the living can't discern what that reason is.

Why is research so important when dealing with ghosts?

Ghosts, like people, have different motivations for acting the way they do. Sometimes their real motives aren't clear because the ghost is behaving in a manner that would lead one to believe the ghost's real goal is different from what it actually is.

For example, in one case I know about, a woman could be seen running and screaming from a particular house every year in the late fall. One might assume that this ghost was an anniversary ghost, and that the day she appeared was the anniversary of her death. This might very well be the case.

This particular house was sold many times over the years with no family staying there more than a year due to the screaming woman. The last time the house was sold, the new owners began renovations on the property. They gutted the house and tore out all the plaster and drywall.

Behind one of the walls of the house, they found the skeleton of a small baby. Of course the owners were horrified and contacted the authorities. The coroner was able to determine that the baby had been dead for a number of years. The townsfolk, having grown up with the story of the screaming woman, assumed the baby belonged to her and insisted that the woman be dug up and the baby be buried with her.

The town paid for this, and as soon as the mother and baby were reunited, the screaming woman wasn't seen again and hasn't been heard from since.

So, while it would have been easy to assume that the screaming woman was an anniversary ghost, the true motivation of this ghost was to have her baby found and to be reunited with it.

Without careful research into the validity of this story and the caring people of this small town, this poor woman would have been destined to spend eternity looking for her baby.

Another prime example is that of a poor spirit, trapped for years in a house, that had the nasty habit of grabbing people and trying to drag them down into the basement.

This behavior scared the people living in the home terribly, and the house was abandoned and fell into disrepair.

A few years ago, when this case came to my attention, my friend and I conducted some basic research on this property and learned that not only had three horse thieves been hanged in one of the barns, but two children had also drowned on the property while playing in a drainage ditch.

This was fascinating, but still did nothing to explain the behavior or identity of the ghost that grabbed anyone who came into the house.

After exhaustive research and after talking to lots of people who had resided in this town for years, we were able to determine that a young couple in their early twenties had lived in the house many years ago. This couple were in the process of a divorce, and one night the husband just disappeared. His wife told people that the man left in the middle of the night and she had no idea where he was.

While on vacation visiting her parents, my friend had the occasion to visit the house for herself. Her older brother, not wanting her to go alone, accompanied her to the house in question. The house stood way out in the middle of nowhere a few miles outside of a small town in Iowa.

They entered the house, and things felt fine until my friend walked into the kitchen. She noticed a door that led to the basement and started to walk toward it. Without warning, something unseen grabbed her around the waist and started to pull her toward the basement door. My friend screamed for her brother. He ran into the kitchen and saw her being pulled toward the basement, but couldn't see what was doing it. He grabbed her arms and pulled her, with much effort, out of the grasp of the spirit. They both fled the house.

Years passed, and due to the physical distance of this house from me and my friend, we were unable to investigate further. However, we heard from one of the people we'd spoken to that in the basement of this house was a sealed cistern. Apparently, someone had gotten curious about the ghost story about this house, which had become somewhat of a legend, and went out to the house and unsealed the cistern. When unsealed, the cistern revealed the skeleton of a man. The coroner determined that the man found in the cistern had been in his early twenties when he'd died of a nasty blow to the head.

So, at first glance one might think the ghost of this poor man was a negative entity who was out to attack and hurt people. But in reality, it was just a ghost desperate to be acknowledged and to have someone find his body. Since the discovery of his body and receiving a proper burial, no one has been attacked at that house.

Without proper research and the curiosity of a citizen of that town, this mystery may have never been solved, and that desperate ghost would have been branded as a negative spirit—or worse, a demon—and never found the peace he so richly deserved.

These examples are classic cases of ghosts behaving in one way, but their motivation for doing so being something totally logical. Just like people, desperate ghosts will take desperate measures to have their story told.

This is why extensive research plays such a vital role in determining why and who may be haunting a particular location.

Do some people want to be haunted?

Sad to say, but the answer is yes. Some people go out of their way to try to summon ghosts, or manifest ghosts out of a common, logical event.

The motivation for wanting to be haunted depends on the people involved. Some people want to feel important or different in some way, while others are just seeking attention.

The problem with this is that such people may be so desperate that they will actually be able not only to draw a ghost into their home, but also to get way more than they bargained for and unwittingly summon a negative entity.

Is it safe to use a Ouija board?

The modern Ouija board was created in 1889 by brothers William and Isaac Fuld. Ouija boards became a fast-selling product in the early twentieth century, when they were marketed as a way to communicate with deceased family members. The Parker Brothers company contacted the children of William Fuld in the 1960s and bought the rights to the Ouija board, after which the company marketed the boards more or less as a game.

There are two lines of thought as to whether the Ouija board is safe to use. Some people believe the Ouija board is nothing but a game, and the movement of the pointer is caused by tiny involuntary movements through your fingers. These people also believe the "messages" received are nothing more than your subconscious being brought forward.

Many paranormal researchers and other people believe the Ouija board is a powerful tool used to communicate with ghosts or other types of entities.

The theory behind this belief is that when using a Ouija board and asking for a spirit or ghost to communicate, what you are really doing is opening a portal to the other side, allowing any type of ghost or entity to come through that door. There is no way to control what comes through the open portal; therefore you could end up with a negative entity, a malevolent ghost, or any number of other things that you don't want in your home.

I can't even remember how many old Victorian-era homes I've been invited to investigate that have unwanted houseguests who have taken up residence and refuse to leave when asked to by the homeowners.

You see, in the early twentieth century the use of talking boards and having a séance were common pastimes and sometimes provided an evening of entertainment for the residents of these homes and their guests. They were seen as a harmless way to pass an evening.

In reality, many ghosts, spirits, and other unwelcome entities were eagerly invited into these houses and not made to leave—if, that is, the occupants of those homes even knew how to deal with such phenomena.

My advice is that you not use a Ouija board, especially if you are already experiencing paranormal activity in your home. The main rule of thumb here is: if you don't know what it is, don't mess with it—which means that if you don't know what type of ghost you have or what it is capable of, don't poke it with a stick to see what it does.

In addition, you could draw some other type of entity into your home through the use of a Ouija board, and therefore make your current situation even worse than it already is. Unless you know how to protect yourself from negative entities, and know how to use a Ouija board properly, I would advise against it.

Can ghosts hurt someone?

While on the surface the answer to this question seems pretty simple, in reality it's complicated because it's a gray area. First you have to define the word *hurt*. Ghosts can take a huge mental toll on a person. If you're living in fear, you may not be sleeping well, you may be more nervous, and you may not be eating like you normally do. Even if the ghost living in your house means no harm to anyone, the fact that you are afraid of it is enough. Living with this mental strain over a period of time can start to affect your health and that of your family.

When dealing with a ghost, fear is the enemy—not the ghost itself. If you or a member of your family is being injured because you are running away from a ghost, then it is not the ghost that is harming you; you are harming yourself. This may seem like a small difference, but if the ghost did nothing to harm you and really means no harm to anyone living, it was your fear that caused you to be injured.

You might be thinking that the ghost, if it meant no harm, should have known you'd be afraid. Remember: the ghost was once a living, breathing person just like yourself and may be desperately trying to make contact with the living.

There have been cases when a ghost or spirit has attacked a living person. Some people who have been victims of such attacks have reported being scratched, punched, and choked, as well as having had objects hurled at them.

Now there are some very nasty ghosts out there, and one of them may decide, for whatever reason, that it doesn't want you or your family in what it considers to be its house and will take drastic actions to send you fleeing from your home.

Little is known about what makes a ghost or spirit evil, but often the answer can be found by researching the history of the house or the place being haunted. It could be that someone was murdered on the property or there were cases of similar violence. It could also be something as simple as the ghost not wanting what it perceives to be trespassers in its home.

Whatever the reason, some of these mean, negative, or downright evil ghosts can be hard to get rid of, and in some cases next to impossible.

There are cases in which objects have been thrown directly at people and in which people have been pushed or tripped on a staircase; in such cases, the answer would be yes, certain types of ghosts can hurt you. A person who was mean and nasty while alive will probably not change when he or she dies and can make your life a living hell.

But again in this situation, fear as well as the ghost is the enemy. The more fear you show toward a ghost of this type, the more it is going to escalate its activity.

The type of entity that is capable of causing the greatest amount of harm to the living is the inhuman, or demon.

Running into an actual demon is extremely rare, despite what you see on television and at the movies.

Inhuman ghosts are capable of unbelievable psychological warfare and physical attacks that can include scratching, biting, pushing, shoving, and so forth.

So as you can see, there is no short answer as to whether a ghost can cause you harm. Most ghosts are harmless, and it is fear that makes some people feel that a ghost is going to hurt them. The important thing to remember is that if you are a witness to paranormal activity, before you react with fear, stop and really think about whether you're being physically or mentally harmed in any way. Chances are you're not.

What is this "dead time" I hear about, and does it really exist?

There are mixed opinions in the world of the paranormal when it comes to "dead time." Some paranormal investigators believe that three a.m. is the time of night when paranormal activity is at its highest. Proponents of this theory believe that because three p.m. is allegedly the time Jesus died, so the opposite would be three a.m. They feel that for this reason, three a.m. is the time most preferred by spirits to become more active.

Another theory is that it's not the ghosts or spirits that are the most active at three in the morning, but that demons are more active at that time because it is the opposite time from when Jesus allegedly died. People who believe in this theory think that demons would go to any length to defy God and Jesus, and that is why demons are the most active at that time.

Whether "dead time" exists or not is up for debate. Personally, I've found ghosts and spirits to be active anytime of the day or night and not to show a preference for one time or another. My feeling is that if a ghost or spirit is present, it's going to be active when it chooses to be active regardless of the time of day or night.

In addition, many people believe in a "Witching Hour." The time this hour occurs, however, varies greatly. Some people believe it is sunset; others, dawn; and still others believe the witching hour is at midnight and other hours during the night.

People who hold to this theory think that the veil or curtain between the world of the living and the realm of the dead are thinnest at whatever hour they believe the witching hour occurs.

Again, I really don't put much stock into the "Witching Hour" theories. The demon I ran across showed no preference for a particular time of day or night to become active, and, at times, was as equally active during the day as it was at night. Although, I have to admit, when the demon did choose to attack, it was always at night, but never at the same time each night.

I believe that at night, our mind and senses can play tricks on us. Everything is quiet, and we may hear noises we wouldn't normally hear during the day. Nights also are, of course, cooler than the daytime because of the lack of sunshine. When wood in particular cools down, it can and does make creaking and/or moaning sounds that could lead many people to believe they are hearing footsteps, or experiencing some other type of paranormal activity.

Nighttime can also play tricks on our eyes, and normal shadows in a room can take on ominous shapes due to many factors. Just last night I could have sworn I saw a shadow dart across the wall in my bedroom. It took me a few moments to realize that my husband had raised up his arms and put them down again in his sleep. Because of the light on the alarm clock, this movement cast an eerie shadow on the wall that appeared to be moving at a rapid rate of speed.

While this event startled me at first, I took the time to look for a logical explanation for what I'd just seen. You can do the same thing with perceived paranormal activity in your home as well. When something startles you, take a second to take a deep breath, calm yourself down, and look for a rational explanation for what just happened. Chances are you will figure it out; if you don't, then you may want to make a note of it in your journal.

Are the urban legends about ghosts true?

In the case of urban legends, it really depends on the legend itself. Many urban legends are based in fact, but over the years they get added to and enhanced until they become practically unrecognizable to the truth.

The legend of the five horsemen is a prime example of an urban legend that has gotten totally out of hand and has caused some people to actually move out of the town because of it.

The story of the five horsemen is set somewhere in the Old West. Out of respect to the town, I'm keeping the exact location private. Anyway, the story goes that five outlaws murdered a family over a land dispute.

Six men from this town and six men from a neighboring town formed a posse and hunted down and killed the horsemen. Less than a year later, one of the towns burned to the ground under what were termed "mysterious circumstances."

The legend says that since the horsemen were killed, they ride through the remaining town, and when they do, people in that small town die.

This legend captured my attention and that of a fellow writer, so we began researching the legend to see what we could find out.

We found the records to the town's cemetery online, and my friend managed to talk to some of the people in this town in order to determine what years the horsemen were reported to have been riding.

After careful review of the cemetery records, we were shocked to discover that during the known years the horsemen rode, more people died than in years when there were either no reported sightings of the horsemen or very few sightings.

The cemetery records turned up another interesting bit of information: most of the people who died in the years the horsemen were known to ride were direct descendents of the twelve men who made up the posse and killed the horsemen.

Does this circumstantial evidence make us think that the horsemen are really killing these people? Absolutely not. Rather, we believe that most of these people are dying from either natural causes or some type of accident. In addition, the median age of the people of this town is sixty-five years old. People die; it happens.

I am more likely to believe that the horsemen have become a convenient excuse for otherwise natural deaths.

The lesson in all this is not to put too much value on urban legends. While they may be born from true events that happened in the past, it would be irrational to think that a ghost associated with an urban legend could haunt your home or, in the extreme, kill someone.

A lot of merchandise on auction sites is advertised as being haunted, especially dolls. Are dolls and all this other merchandise really haunted?

Some of the merchandise on these auction sites can be haunted, although I doubt all of it is. There are many people who collect "haunted" items and have huge collections of it, although the logic behind that eludes me.

It is highly possible for a ghost or another type of entity to attach itself to a particular object, such as a doll, for example. Items like religious icons, statues, and other devotional objects have been reported to be charged with energy that some people believe to be a ghost of a departed loved one or a divine being such as an angel.

It is very common to find that most paranormal and haunted objects are antiques. This is because it can take a period of years for enough energy to build up to the point that the object can be considered "haunted." Also, in this case, haunted does not necessarily mean occupied by a ghost.

The majority of objects that are reported to be haunted really aren't, but they may be storing a large amount of energy they have gathered over time. The theory is that everything on Earth is composed of some form of energy and that matter in any form is composed of various waves and frequencies, not unlike radio waves.

This theory goes on to state that we are each affecting everything around us, through our thoughts, actions, and movements. This is called *resonance*, and is a completely natural event that occurs every day in our world.

When the human soul leaves its body, it is still able to affect things on Earth if it chooses to. So haunted objects have simply retained the energy of the people who once owned them, through resonance, which again is a perfectly natural phenomenon.

If an object is truly haunted, then there is a trapped, confused, and possibly unfriendly spirit residing in that object. These spirits do not have the power to grant wishes or bring you wealth, no matter what some of the people selling them advertise. Think about it: if an object could bring wealth and grant wishes, then why is someone selling it?

I want to say a few more words about haunted dolls. If you buy your child a doll at a garage sale, thrift store, or online auction site, and your child doesn't play with it often or tells you he or she is afraid of it, listen to your kid. Children can feel this type of thing more easily than adults can, and chances are if your child is telling you there is something wrong with that doll, then there is.

Get that doll or any other object you suspect may be haunted out of your home as soon as possible. While I understand that some people collect haunted objects, I can't figure out why someone would invite that type of potential danger into their home. There is no way to tell what type of ghost is trapped in the object, and you could get a whole lot more trouble than you ever bargained for.

Can ghosts appear in our dreams?

Yes! It would not be unusual to have a spirit of a departed loved one appear to you in your dreams. If you have dreamt that you were having a conversation with a family member or close friend who passed away, chances are you probably were.

You may dream that the person was sitting on the end of your bed, or somewhere in your bedroom, although other scenarios are common as well.

The reason some ghosts choose to appear to us in dreams is so we won't be scared. Just because our loved ones are dead does not mean that the emotions and person they used to be do not follow them in death. They realize that if they appeared to you while you were awake, it would scare you.

If they come to you in a dream, you will not be afraid, because your brain will treat it the same way as it does a dream and not trigger the fear response. When you wake up in the morning, you may think you had a dream about your loved one and comment on how real it seemed. In fact, you may have been visited by your loved one who has passed and shared a few wonderful moments with this person.

Keep in mind that a visitation by your family member or friend who passed away is different from just having a dream about this person. In a visitation, everything will be in place and nothing will seem odd or unrealistic. In the usual type of dream we normally have, things may seem disjointed or move either very fast or very slow. Events and objects in these "normal" dreams may seem "wrong" somehow or out of place.

The morning after you've had a dream about your loved one, think about the dream and see if you can distinguish if it was really "just a dream" or instead if it was a visitation by someone near and dear to you.

What is hypnagogia?

The word *hypnagogia* describes the period of time when your body is just about to fall asleep. Many people report bizarre experiences during this time. Some people have reported the feeling of being held down on their bed unable to breathe or move, as though there is a strong pressure on their chest. It's also been reported by certain people that they've heard footsteps or someone talking to them, had the feeling of floating, or saw lights, shadows, or people in their room.

What is an EVP?

EVP stands for *electronic voice phenomenon*. One of the first experimenters with electronic voice phenomena was Thomas Edison. He spent the last years of his life experimenting with recording the voices of ghosts.

Because it is a common belief in the paranormal world that ghosts are made up of energy and magnetism, the same things used when recording audio into a tape recorder, it makes perfect sense that a ghost could communicate with the living using a tape recorder.

Normally an EVP will be one or two words long or a short sentence, and I have not heard of anyone capturing a complete paragraph or having a meaningful conversation with a spirit through the use of a tape recorder. Yet the phenomenon is fascinating, and new devices are being invented all the time to try to improve the communication abilities of a spirit to the living.

Are there ways a ghost can communicate with us other than through an EVP?

Yes. Ghosts try to communicate with us in many different ways. They may make noise to get our attention; they can appear as an apparition; and they can cause odors to appear in a room that may or may not remind us of the person the ghost once was.

Ghosts might also leave a small gift of something they owned when they were alive where you can easily find it. You may get chills, get touched, or receive a hug.

In some cases, you could have what you perceive to be a dream of the person in which you carry on an entire conversation with your loved one who has passed.

Lights in your home might go on and off; the telephone or doorbell may ring and no one's there; or you could see an impression on a piece of furniture as if someone were sitting on it.

Sometimes a spirit might hide some of your personal items or move them to another location in order to get your attention. You may even see some objects move around your home, although that would be a very extreme case.

There have been instances in which a person has received a telephone call from the dead. This phenomenon happened to my daughter. She'd been living in my parents' condominium after my father died and my mother went to an assisted living facility.

My daughter called me one day in a panic after she got home from work. My late father had left a message on the answering machine! She played the message back for me, and it was definitely my father's voice saying, "Alice, oh my God, Alice." Alice was my mother's name.

I have to admit, while it did freak me out a little bit, it was exhilarating at the same time! I mean, to actually be witness to such an event was a huge thrill. Although at the same time it made me wonder if he was okay.

I came to the conclusion that he was fine, and just hanging around the condominium occasionally because my daughter was living there.

What is a vortex?

Many paranormal researchers believe that a vortex is the point of entry and exit from one dimension to another. For example, it is the point in your home or business where ghosts can pass from the world of the living to the other side.

Some people claim to have photographed vortexes, and I've seen pictures of a white mist rotating like a top and making a swirling pattern. Does that mean these are pictures of a vortex? I can't say for sure, but it would be a logical conclusion one could jump to.

Can pets come back as ghosts?

Yes, it is very common for your pets to come back to visit or comfort you after they have died. You may hear familiar sounds that were associated with your pet; you may see the misty image of your pet; and in some cases you may see an indentation on the pet's bed or your bed, wherever that pet slept.

While no one is really sure if other animals come back as ghosts, it is widely believed that pets come back because of the strong emotional bonds they had with their human companions.

Ghosts of animals have been witnessed on battlefields, as well as many other places, but the most common place is in a home soon after a pet has died.

Some people have reported hearing the ghost of their dog growling if someone gets too close, and even the United States Capitol building is allegedly haunted by the ghost of a cat that appears out of the shadows with glowing eyes and startles people.

It's not uncommon to hear the purring of a ghost cat sleeping on your bed and seeing an indentation in the bed covers where it's resting.

As an example, soon after my beloved golden retriever, Bear, was put to sleep due to bone cancer, I walked into our master bathroom and saw Bear lying on the tile floor. He raised his head and looked at me before vanishing into thin air. When alive, Bear had always loved to sleep on the cool tile of the bathroom floor.

On another occasion, I was in bed sick with the flu. I couldn't sleep and was watching some television. I distinctly felt Bear jump on the bed and lie down with his head on my stomach as he'd done every night of his life. We had a waterbed, and when the ghost of Bear jumped on it, he caused a big wave before he settled down next to me. It was very comforting, even if I couldn't physically see him.

What are ley lines, and do they affect paranormal activity?

Ley lines are made up of a grid of the earth's energy that runs around the planet. It is believed that ancient people were aware of these lines and built their monuments and sometimes their temples where they felt the ley lines had some significance. Stonehenge is a prime example of this. There are ley lines that run through Stonehenge, and the people who built it didn't put it there by accident.

As for ley lines and paranormal activity: a few years ago paranormal researchers would have scoffed at such an idea, but things are changing. Some people believe that there are negative and positive ley lines in order to maintain a balance.

A negative ley line could make someone feel uneasy or just "not feel right." Does this mean that there is a negative spirit or ghost there? Not at all. It is just the human body reacting to the negative energy from that particular ley line.

While we're on the subject of the geopathic, many people believe that poltergeist activity or other forms of paranormal activity are stronger if there's water nearby. The water could be in the form of a lake, an old well, an underground stream, or any other place water can and does accumulate.

Still others believe that the effects of water lines on the human body and brain could play a large role in why some people perceive paranormal activity to be more prevalent near a water line.

Many people who have stood over a known water line have reported feeling a heaviness in different parts of their body, particularly in their extremities such as their arms and legs. Others have felt like they are standing in syrup, or have experienced a slow and warm feeling.

Water lines and ley lines can affect people in different ways. So, it would stand to reason that because ley lines and water lines are a form of energy, they could affect the behavior of ghosts as well because ghosts are made up of energy.

It's also a possibility that paranormal activity could be increased if you live near a ley line. Because it's widely accepted that ghosts and spirits are made up of energy, and ley lines are composed of energy, then a ghost or spirit could be more attracted to a large energy source.

Everything a ghost or spirit does requires energy. It needs energy to move objects, slam doors, and so on. Normally a ghost would draw the energy it needs from the people around; it's entirely possible that if a ghost is by a ley line, it would have an unlimited amount of energy to draw off of and therefore would be able to be more active, which, logically, would increase the amount of paranormal activity in that area.

Are there different types of spirit guides?

Many people believe so, and some people use the terms *guardians* and *angels* to describe their guides. Some of the most common spirit guides are *ancestral guides*, who are family members who have died. Followers of many religions may see an ancestral guide as their guardian angel.

A *teacher guide* generally will not be a constant companion throughout your life, but rather will show up at certain times when needed. For example, a teacher guide may show up to help you solve a problem or to provide insight, and then move on.

Animal guides, in some belief systems such as among some Native Americans, are there to teach and protect us. At the same time, some people believe that an animal guide is there more to be a companion than to actually fulfill some higher purpose.

CHAPTER 9

What's a Person to Do, or Not Do, as the Case May Be?

*M*uch has been written and shown on television about how to get rid of spirits or ghosts that have taken up residence in a person's home. Some of it I agree with, some of it . . . not so much. It's been my experience that every situation is different and must be dealt with based upon the activity and the temperament of the spirit.

That being said, let's look at a few different methods of possibly removing a spirit from your home. Please remember that none of the techniques in this chapter are guaranteed to work, and the time may come when you need to call in help.

With most of these techniques for ridding your home of ghosts, it is the intent behind the words you speak that is so important. In other words, you must truly believe in what you are doing and what you're saying in order for any of these methods to be effective.

Residual Haunting

If you've been able to determine that you are experiencing a residual haunting, there's really nothing you can do. You have two choices: you can realize that there really isn't a ghost there, that it's a piece of energy caught in time and will eventually fade away; or you can choose to move. While this may seem a bit harsh, it's the truth. Remember: no one is being harmed.

Because a residual haunting does not involve a ghost but a piece of time caught in some type of time continuum, there is no other course of action but to let it run its course. It is important to realize, and it can't be stressed enough, that in a residual haunting there is no ghost present; hence, there is nothing to get rid of.

The activity surrounding a residual haunting can be frightening and scary, but in my experience, once you know exactly what you're dealing with, the fear goes away.

Traditional/Intelligent Haunting

As you've read in previous chapters, there are many different types of ghosts that can be present in an intelligent haunting situation. The methods to get rid of these ghosts are generally the same. Let's take a look at some of the most common ways to get rid of an unwanted houseguest.

Talk to It

As simple as this sounds, talking to the ghost is generally the easiest way either to have the ghost leave or at least reach some type of compromise to cohabitate. It is also the first thing I recommend to all my clients.

If you believe the spirit could be that of a previous owner of your home, you can say something like, "I understand you loved your home and don't want to leave it. But it's our home now, and we will take very good care of it. You don't have to worry anymore, and you can go into the light and join your family on the other side now."

Keep in mind you may have to repeat yourself many times and make the message a little stronger each time. This does not guarantee the ghost will leave, but it's the best place to start.

Remember that some ghosts don't know they're dead, and you may have to nicely explain to them that they no longer belong in the world of the living and it will be much better for them if they go into the light or cross over to the other side.

After a few days or weeks of nicely asking the ghost to leave with no results, you can escalate your message to something like *"This is our house and you are not wanted here! You need to get out now! Leave!"* You can also use this technique for other types of ghosts that you feel may be negative.

The most important thing to do is be firm in your tone and manner. There is no need to yell and scream at the entity in order to get your point across. A ghost will not take you seriously if you act scared and frightened. Be assertive and proactive in reclaiming your home.

If you really don't mind the ghost in your home, but just wish it would not walk the floors at three a.m., then set ground rules and boundaries.

You could say, "We really don't mind if you're here, but could you please not go into the children's rooms?" You can substitute whatever you want the ghost to do or not do.

As strange as this may sound, it does work and is your first line of defense in getting rid of unwanted ghosts or at the very least coming to an agreement.

A ghost or spirit may be afraid of being judged, or afraid of some type of punishment being exacted on it for things it did while alive. If you think that the entity you're dealing with might be experiencing this fear, you may want to tell the spirit that you understand these feelings, but that if they do leave, they will be treated with love and kindness, and will be forgiven for any actions and behaviors that happened while alive.

Have You Done Any Shopping Lately?

If the paranormal activity occurring in your home is rather recent, think about any items you may have purchased lately. It could be items from a thrift store, eBay, a garage sale, or an antique store. Anything that you bought secondhand could have a ghost attached to it.

Something as small as that toy car you bought at a garage sale for your son, or that doll you picked up at the thrift store for your daughter—any item large or small could have a ghost attached to it.

Once you determine what you've bought recently, try to figure out if the paranormal activity was happening before you bought that item or after. If it's after you bought that particular item, try getting rid of the item, and I don't mean put it in the basement, garage, or shed. I mean get it off your property.

Once the item or items are removed from your home, pay attention and see if the paranormal activity stops. If it does: problem solved.

Have Your Home Blessed

If the spirit in your home is persistent, you may want to have a trusted member of clergy come into your home and bless the space. Some people are nervous to ask their church for help with such things, for fear of having their sanity questioned.

Instead of having your home blessed, you can select a few small objects from your home and ask a member of the clergy to bless them without saying why. Once these objects are blessed, place one in each room.

If you are uncomfortable having a member of the clergy bless your home or objects, or if you are not particularly religious, you can try blessing the home yourself. It's important that you pay particular attention to all doors, windows, the kitchen, and the bedrooms. Also pay close attention to any other rooms where paranormal activity may have occurred at one time.

You can burn sage incense or dried sage in every room of the house one at a time and repeat this simple house blessing in every room:

> *Please bless this house and fill it with only positive energy, happiness, love, and peace. Anyone who enters this space can only be someone who is filled with love and happiness. Any negative energy or beings can no longer reside within these walls, and they are to leave and are forbidden to enter this home again. This room is hereby blessed and filled with only love, peace, and happiness.*

You may have to repeat this process more than once. Don't forget to do the attic and the basement. Negative spirits can hide in many places in your home, and the goal is to give them no safe place anymore, so they will be forced to leave.

Use Holy Water

You can take a small, clean container with a lid and respectfully go to a church and fill it with holy water. When you have the holy water, go around your house and put a bit of holy water on your finger and make the sign of the cross on every door frame.

When you make the cross with the holy water, you can say, "I bless and clean this space in the name of the Lord" or any other prayer you wish. If you are not particularly religious, you may want to say a mantra that goes, "I order any spirits in this space to leave."

The trick to completing this task properly is to really believe with all your heart what you're doing and saying. So if you are not comfortable with saying a prayer, use a mantra, and vice versa. Be firm and assertive in your tone. There's no need to yell, but if you project a calm, assertive energy and truly mean what you're saying, the use of holy water can be very effective in ridding your home of spirits.

Pray to Whomever You Believe In

Whether you believe in God, the Goddess, Buddha, Allah, or if you simply want to pray to your ancestors or family members who have passed away, when dealing with a spirit it can't hurt to enlist the help of loving spirits who may be able to help the ghost find its way to the other side or be effective in convincing it to leave you alone.

Smudging

Smudging is a Native American technique that has proven to be very effective for ridding homes of uninvited ghosts. If you are a person of faith, it is perfectly acceptable for you to say prayers during the time you go through the smudging process.

To smudge your home, you can either purchase smudging sticks online, or you can use a mixture of dried sage and sweet grass. Sometimes sweet grass is hard to find, so you can also use incense instead of sweet grass and/or sage with the same effect.

If you're using incense, place the incense in a small bowl and light it. Blow out any flame so you have only smoke. If you're using a smudge stick or dried sage, do the same thing. The important thing is that you have only smoke and no flame.

Crack open one window in each room. Starting at one end of your house, walk through every room making sure the smoke from the incense gets into all the corners and nooks and crannies. You can use a large feather if you want so you can direct the smoke into every corner of the room.

While you're doing each room, you can say a prayer or you can say something to the effect of, " This smoke is cleaning out any negative energy or spirits. All negative energy or spirits are commanded to leave now through the open window and are never to return. I am clearing this house of any negative energy. You must leave."

Once you've smudged every room in the house, go back through and shut all the windows.

You may have to repeat the smudging process a few times at once-a-week intervals before the ghost gets the message and gets out. This method is not magic, Wicca, or witchcraft. It is simply a technique that can be effective in ridding a home of spirits.

Light a White Candle

Some people believe that this method works and have had success with it. Personally I've never tried it, but I would be interested to hear anyone's results.

Take a white candle into a room and light it. Make sure you use a new candle, not one that has already been burned. Walk around the room with the candle lit and order any ghosts or any negative entities out of your home. Repeat this same process in every room.

The theory is that the white candle represents divine energy and that the lit candle—along with your calm, assertive words ordering a ghost out—will drive a ghost from your home.

There is no guarantee any of these methods will work, but the mere fact that you are taking action and refusing to live in fear will go a long way in reclaiming your home.

Feng Shui

Some paranormal researchers swear by feng shui to get rid of any negative energy or spirit that occupies a home. You can try rearranging your furniture to change the energy of a room, burn incense, or purchase a small oil diffuser. There are many good books on feng shui. The theory behind feng shui is that by clearing out clutter, changing furniture around, and using certain colors, you are inviting in only positive energy and that negative energy can't dwell in such a space. Feng shui experts also recommend playing music to raise the vibrations of the space.

I've never tried feng shui to clear a home of unwanted spirits or energy, but it would definitely be worth a try.

Protecting Your Children

As I mentioned in chapter 5, your children may become frightened by the presence of a ghost in your home or could experience the ghost being in their room. This is not only very scary for them, but, as a parent myself, I also know you worry about your children and their safety.

If your kids are just being scared but not harmed by the ghost, there is a very easy and fun thing you and your children can do together to make them feel more secure and perhaps keep the ghost from entering their bedroom.

Make angels with your children. Gather together some construction paper or cloth, scissors, glue, and anything you and your children want to decorate the angels with, such as sequins, glitter, feathers, and the like. Make enough angels so that one can go on the outside of their bedroom door, one on the inside of their bedroom door, and one each in their closet, at the foot of their beds, and at the head of the beds.

While you and your children are making the angels, talk with them about how whatever supreme being you believe in protects children and keeps them safe. Make it fun!

Once the angels are completed, hang them in the appropriate places in their bedroom and on the doors, both inside and out.

I want to make this very clear: this is not witchcraft, Wicca, or any other type of magic. I can't explain why this works, but I do know that in many cases it does work. I've used it with my own grandchildren, and on cases I've handled in which children were involved, with relatively great success.

However, if your child is being harmed in any manner, don't even hesitate to get help immediately. Small children and most teenagers are not emotionally or mentally equipped to deal with any form of entity and can easily be preyed upon by some types of ghosts, spirits, and other beings.

Folklore and Old Wives' Tales on How to Get Rid of a Ghost

There are many stories in different cultures about how to ward off or get rid of ghosts. I haven't tried any of these, but I have an open mind and am interested to see if these home remedies really work.

If you try one of the suggestions listed below and have success with it, please let me know! I'd be very happy to hear what you tried and what your results were.

Hazelnuts

Many cultures have been using hazelnuts for centuries, and their use for ridding places of unwanted ghosts has been around since ancient times. The Pagans used hazelnuts during Samhain, often referred to as the Great Gathering. They would put nine hazelnuts on a string and burn them over the fire, while saying: "Hazelnuts, nine in a ring/By the smoke of the Samhain fire bring/Protection to this house and those within/Blessed be this charm of nuts and string."

They believed this would protect them from negative forces in the universe. This tradition, handed down through generations, has been changed several times by various religions to fit in with their belief systems, but the meaning stayed the same.

You can either string the hazelnuts together and hang them on your door, or add some other decorations. Whatever you do with them, just make sure you hang them on any door that goes in and out of your home.

If you're particularly religious, you can ask a trusted member of the clergy to bless the hazelnuts as a bit of added protection.

Give the Ghosts Something to Count

Many cultures around the world believe that if you give a ghost a seemingly impossible task, the ghost will give up and leave.

Some people sprinkle a cupful of rice or sand on the floor of the haunted rooms every night before they go to bed. The belief is that the ghost will stop to count the granules, and after a few nights will tire of this impossible task and simply leave. Clean up the mess the next morning, and repeat it every night until the haunting stops.

Because variations of this home remedy for ghosts are so prevalent in different cultures, there may be something to it, and it certainly would be worth a try.

Garlic

According to folklore, garlic isn't just to repel vampires anymore. The folklore of many cultures says that if you hang or lay a clove of garlic by each window and door, it will make the ghosts go away.

I'm not too sure about this one, but it won't hurt to try it. If any of you do try this, I'd be very interested in your results.

Mixed-Up Shoes

Of all the home remedies I've read about, one of my favorites for getting rid of ghosts is to put the shoes you're going to wear the next day on the floor at the end of your bed, with one shoe facing one way and the other one facing in the opposite direction. The story goes that this will confuse a ghost so much that it will leave after a few nights.

I have no idea if this will work, but in my experience stories like this do not last for centuries without some merit and truth behind them, so give it a shot. It certainly can't hurt anything or make the activity worse.

What Not to Do

Now that we've covered the basics of what to do in an attempt to rid your home of a ghost, it's time to discuss what *not* to do.

Do Not Show Fear

I completely understand that this is easier said than done, but some types of ghosts feed off your fear and become stronger and more powerful. Your fear can actually escalate the activity in your home. It's always best to try to remain calm and take an assertive approach by ordering the ghost out of your house.

If you are a religious person, try envisioning a holy being standing next to you and protecting you from the ghost. You could also try a prayer to whatever religious figure you worship—including one of your guides or angels, depending on what you believe—and asking for their help and protection.

Do Not Use Salt; Try Rice Instead

I know, I know: everyone is telling you to put a line of sea salt around the outside of your home, or to put it on windowsills and in small bowls throughout the house.

However, if you already have a ghost inside your home, putting salt around your home is the last thing you want to do.

The theory is that spirits can't cross a line of sea salt. So if you already have a ghost inside your house, then by putting sea salt around the outside of your house or on the windowsills and by doors, you are trapping the ghost inside your home and preventing it from leaving! Not the result you want.

Instead of salt, use rice. Sprinkle a line of rice around the outside perimeter of your home, getting the rice as close to the foundation of your home as possible. The theory behind this is that rice will lure the spirit out of your house. I haven't tried this personally, but I have heard from reputable people in the paranormal field that this can work.

Once you are sure the ghost is gone from your home, then it is safe to put a line of sea salt around the outside of your home to prevent any more negative ghosts or spirits from entering.

Do Not Use a Ouija Board or Have a Séance

Ouija boards and séances are tools that are used to invite ghosts or other types of spirits into the world of the living and into your home.

If you attempt one of these things, and it works, you could wind up with more ghosts—or, even worse, an inhuman spirit in your house.

Ouija boards and séances, when they work, are opening a door to the other side, and anything can come through that door. There is no way to control an open gateway to the other side.

For example, every year on Devil's Night, the night before Halloween, my cousin used to have a Halloween party on her farm. I was in my early twenties and attended one of those parties. After everyone ate and had a few drinks, we all went out into the barn to hold a séance.

My cousin was very well aware of my abilities and asked me to lead the séance, which I did. We lit candles, sat down on the floor of the barn in a circle, and all held hands. After the opening ceremony, we asked if anyone was with us.

Within a few moments, the person sitting across from me gasped and her eyes got really big. I turned my head around and saw the shadow of a huge sickle swinging like a pendulum on the back wall of the barn.

It didn't take long for everyone to see the same shadow swinging ominously, and I immediately ordered the circle broken and the lights to be turned on in the barn. After all that, the shadow of the sickle remained. We checked the barn and there wasn't a real sickle anywhere around.

My cousin reported it took almost two days for that shadow to disappear. Her horses and other animals refused to enter the barn. Once the shadow was gone, the animals had no problem returning to the barn.

If any paranormal researcher or ghost hunter informs you they plan to use a Ouija board or hold a séance in your home, tell them that is not acceptable and find a different ghost hunter to work with. If the ghost hunter you work with doesn't tell you he or she plans on using these techniques, and then starts a séance or begins to use a Ouija board, tell this ghost hunter to stop immediately and order the ghost hunter out of your house.

If you currently own a Ouija board, *do not* burn it. Some people believe that by burning a Ouija board you will be bringing a curse upon your family or home. People may tell you to burn a Ouija board, but in reality you should bury the board somewhere off your property.

It is highly recommended that you break or cut the Ouija board into seven pieces, sprinkle it with holy water, and bury it somewhere peaceful and not on your own property.

Take it out into the country, away from towns or people, and bury it in the woods or some other appropriate place.

Conclusion

Throughout history, people have come up with interesting and creative ways to get rid of unwanted ghosts and spirits. Some methods to rid a place of ghosts may work one time and then not work the next. There's no rhyme or reason to what will work when. I believe this is due to the fact that, like people, ghosts and spirits each have their own individual personalities.

In the next chapter, we will talk about when to get help and how to select a good ghost-hunting group, or paranormal research team, to come into your home.

CHAPTER 10

When and Where to Get Help

If you believe you're unable to get rid of the ghost in your home, then you may want to seek the assistance of a ghost-hunting group or paranormal research team. Keep in mind that not all ghost-hunting groups are created equal, and you need to be picky when choosing a group to let into your house.

Also, not many ghost-hunting groups are equipped to get rid of ghosts. Ghost hunters study the paranormal, and, while they may be able to help you identify the type of ghost, and in some cases narrow down the list of whom the ghost may have been when alive, most ghost-hunting teams do not get rid of ghosts.

Some ghost-hunting teams may be able to direct you to someone who can smudge your home for you or bless your home. Other ghost-hunting teams may have a medium that can make contact with the spirit.

I do want to address the issue of the use of mediums in these types of situations. Being a medium myself, I know how effective they can be in assisting a team of paranormal researchers.

That being said, not all mediums are legitimate and some of them claim to see evil or demons wherever they go. I'm not telling you to dismiss a medium as a fraud; I'm simply asking you to be a little skeptical until the medium proves his or her worth.

If the ghost-hunting team you choose has a medium on their team, they should make you aware of it. With our team, I am simply there to help find the "hot spots" (the places where I feel the most energy, or possibility for catching paranormal activity). Our team does not rely on what I tell them I pick up or "feel." We rely on any scientific evidence we capture to determine whether a location is haunted or not. Most legitimate paranormal researchers operate in the same manner.

Occasionally, I will "pick up" other information, but this information is not taken as the truth until we can verify it with scientific evidence or intensive historical research.

More on how to select a proper ghost-hunting team will be discussed later in this chapter. For now we're going to concentrate on when to get help for you and your family.

When to Seek Help

Physical Attacks

If you or anyone in your family is being physically harmed by a ghost, you will want to get help as soon as possible. Some negative ghosts are capable of scratching, punching, pushing, shoving, biting, and other forms of physical abuse.

There is no reason to tolerate this type of behavior from anyone, especially a ghost. Some negative ghosts may use physical violence to terrorize and intimidate you and chase you from your home.

Sometimes a very stern verbal message will make this activity stop, but in more cases than not, it won't. Physical violence from a ghost is very rare, but it can and does happen.

I had a case in which a ghost tried to push me and a few others down a flight of stairs. As soon as I headed up that staircase, I could sense the ghost lying in wait at the top of the stairs. I simply ordered him to back off and not even try it. The ghost complied, and no one was ever pushed down that staircase again. In fact, that ghost and I actually became pretty good friends later in the investigation. As I said at the beginning of this book, weird is pretty much my normal.

Children Being Threatened

One thing I cannot tolerate is a child being threatened or harmed in any way. Because children are more open to the paranormal, they tend to experience it more often than many adults.

If your child is being threatened or harmed in any manner by a ghost, then you should seek help immediately.

It's perfectly normal for a child to be scared of such activity, but you want to make sure your child is not being physically, mentally, or emotionally harmed by a ghost.

A lot depends on the age of the child as well. While all children should be protected and kept safe, younger children do not have the coping skills or life experiences to emotionally and logically deal with a ghost. Teenagers and older children generally are able to cope with a ghost more easily, unless they are being attacked physically or feel they are being threatened by a ghost.

Most reputable paranormal groups will respond almost immediately if a child in involved. I know our team does. Any case involving a child automatically goes to the top of the list.

When You've Just Had Enough

There may come a time when you've tried everything, or are simply too frightened to take any action because of the paranormal activity occurring in your home. This is totally understandable. Living with some types of ghosts can be very stressful and overwhelming.

If this is the situation you are in, don't hesitate to contact either me or a good ghost-hunting team in your area for assistance.

How to Find a Good Ghost Hunter

As I said before, not all ghost-hunting teams are created equal. There are many groups out there that don't take what they do seriously, or are completely unprofessional. So to make things easier for you, I've created a list of what you want to look for in a ghost-hunting or paranormal research team.

Phone Number

Most ghost-hunting groups do not list a telephone number on their website. This is to prevent getting numerous prank phone calls at all hours of the day and night.

Generally there will be a form to fill out online or an e-mail address you can use to contact a member of the group. This is perfectly acceptable.

However, once initial contact has been made, you will want to have a phone number of someone you can contact should an emergency arise. While this won't guarantee the credibility of the ghost-hunting team, it will help to weed out the ghost-hunter wannabes.

The Website

Anyone can have a website, and there are many places on the Internet to get free websites. What you want to do before contacting any team is to look at the ghost hunters' website carefully.

See if it lists the investigators' names. If it doesn't, chances are this group is not serious about what they do, and are only looking for fun.

Remember: websites are a form of advertising, so look through the website and determine if the members of this group are people you'd like to invite into your home. The website should contain good, quality material.

If a ghost-hunting group offers "magical" cleanings of your home or offers to use magic to help you, move on. Most paranormal researchers do not employ these methods. When you speak to someone from any ghost-hunting team, make sure and ask them about this.

Fees

Legitimate ghost hunters do not charge for their services. If anyone asks you to pay for an investigation, then look for someone else. If, however, the group is out of state or needs to travel overnight to reach your location, you should offer to pay for their travel expenses.

Qualifications

Once you find a ghost-hunting team you feel comfortable with, ask them about their qualifications. Find out how long they have been investigating paranormal activity, and what types of cases they have done in the past. Don't be afraid to ask the paranormal investigators for references from past clients. They may not give you any, and that would be okay, too. Many people want to remain private, but I've had clients who will let me use them as a reference, so it's still a good idea to ask for references.

Be a little skeptical if someone has a "doctor" in their name. Ask where they received their doctorate, and what the doctorate is in. People can buy doctorates on the Internet or obtain them from an online university, but that doesn't mean they are qualified to conduct a paranormal investigation.

What Happens During an Investigation

Once you've figured out which ghost hunters you feel most comfortable with, they will have to determine whether an on-site investigation is warranted. In order to do this, they will have to ask you questions—a lot of them.

If they determine they need to have their team come out to your home to conduct an investigation, you should know that ghost-hunting investigations are very invasive.

A good team will take hundreds of photographs and run video cameras almost everywhere. All your statements will be recorded, and you will be asked to walk a few of the investigators through the house and describe in detail all of the events that have occurred.

If possible, have a copy of your journal and any research ready to give them. This will greatly increase the possibility of a positive result to the investigation.

Try to bear with their seemingly endless questions. Each question has a purpose, and your answers will help them determine what type of activity is occurring and the type of ghost that could be causing it.

A professional ghost-hunting team will approach each investigation with a healthy dose of skepticism. Not because they don't believe you, but because they want to try to determine if there is a logical and/or reasonable explanation for the events you are experiencing.

The ghost hunters may come in with what seems like a ton of equipment: video cameras, tape recorders, computers, EMF detectors, and wireless DVR cameras. If you don't understand something, don't be afraid to ask. Good investigators should be able to explain to you what they are doing, what the equipment is, and why it is necessary for this investigation.

Try to have all people who witnessed the events either be present in person or be available by telephone to answer any questions the investigators may have. Please keep any other friends or relatives away from the house the night of the investigation, and small children should be sent to a friend's or relative's home to spend the night. Too many people can be distracting and can interfere with the investigation.

If at any point you become uncomfortable with the investigation process, you do have the right to ask them to stop the investigation. The investigators are guests in your home.

Every professional investigator will follow up with you after the investigation. Be patient with this process; it can take days of tedious work to review hours of video, audio, and photographs.

As a general rule, there should be no more than six to eight investigators in your home at one time. Sometimes, depending on the size of a location, more investigators may be required, but generally a small team works best in a residential situation.

None of the investigators should be drinking or engaging in rowdy behavior while investigating your home.

If the investigation was set up through one of your local television stations or newspapers, the ghost-hunting team should never show up with a production crew or reporter without your express permission before the investigation even begins.

A professional ghost-hunting team will keep all aspects of your case confidential unless you give them permission to put their findings on their website or in print media. Many times a ghost-hunting team will have you sign a release, which will allow you to choose what type of information can be used by the ghost-hunting team, if any. This is perfectly acceptable, and most ghost-hunting teams will keep your name and the location private, but want to show any evidence they got during the investigation to others. This is also perfectly acceptable, depending on how comfortable you feel doing this.

If, in reviewing the journal you've kept, a pattern emerges, the ghost hunters will want to have a vigil that coincides with the established pattern of activity. This vigil can be very long, protracted, and boring for both you and the investigators.

Many times, more than one investigation may be needed in order to determine whether your home is haunted, not haunted, or just experiencing some form of paranormal activity. A second ghost hunt in your home is a lot less invasive than the first.

What Should Happen After an Investigation

Any paranormal investigation team should not just do their investigation and then disappear, with you never hearing from them again or them not returning any of your telephone calls or e-mails.

Find out before you let a team of ghost hunters into your home what services they provide to you after they've conducted their investigation.

A good paranormal investigation team should meet with you within a relatively short period of time after the investigation to go over any evidence they got and explain to you how they got the evidence, where in your home the evidence was found, and, most importantly, how they can help you rid your home of an unwanted ghost or spirit.

Keep in mind that it can take several days to a couple of weeks for a paranormal investigation team to carefully review the hours and hours of videotape, audio, and photographs they took.

Once the information gathered is reviewed, every bit of evidence needs to be double-checked and put together. It's almost like a puzzle, with the pieces being witness statements, any personal experiences members of the ghost-hunting team may have had during the investigation, and any hard evidence they caught during the time they were in your home.

All this data should be assimilated into one cohesive theory about what types of ghosts or spirits are occupying your home or place of business, if any; whether a logical explanation can be found to explain some the activity reported; and what type of haunting you're experiencing. It's also possible that while you may be experiencing some paranormal activity, the activity may not be consistent enough to say for sure your home is haunted.

Remember: an actual haunting is extremely rare, but you still could be experiencing some paranormal activity. As discussed previously, not only does an actual haunting need to have consistent activity, but there also has to be a ghost or spirit that either interacts, or attempts to interact, in some way with the living.

Conclusion

If you choose to contact a ghost-hunting team or paranormal investigator, don't be afraid to interview more than one until you find the person you feel most comfortable with. Remember that you're going to be inviting these people into your home.

Don't hesitate to ask for an initial meeting with just one or two of the team members. One of those members should be one of the founders of the group. If the founder of the group can't take the time to meet with you, you may want to reconsider using that group.

If after the initial meeting you are not comfortable with the people for any reason, then move on to a different team of ghost hunters or paranormal investigators.

Unless it is an absolute emergency, my team tries to do a little historical research before going out on an investigation—not only on the property we're going to be investigating, but also on the area and town surrounding the location.

There's a lot to be learned by taking the time to research before an investigation begins. On one occasion in particular, we discovered by talking to the current owners of the property and doing some research that the property once was a general store and train station, and that train tracks used to run through their backyard.

This research went a long way in explaining some of the paranormal activity we recorded during the investigation. We were able to distinguish what was residual energy and what was an intelligent ghost or spirit while reviewing our tapes.

CHAPTER 11

The Bottom Line

So we've made it this far, and I hope you've found the information in this book helpful. I've tried to put the material into the most useful order for you, so that you can become armed with the knowledge you need to determine if you have paranormal activity in your home and what to do about it.

But now that we're at the last chapter of this book and it's just you and me, I'm going to talk to you just like I'd talk to one of my friends. In other words, here's the bottom line the way I see it as it pertains to the world of the paranormal.

When it comes to ghosts and spirits, I can say they exist. I've seen them, been touched by them, and have spent most of my adult life dealing with them in one way or another. I've found that there are good ghosts and bad ghosts, and that they aren't much different from us, except they are in spirit form and not in a human body.

I've spent a great deal of time helping the ghosts while also helping the people whose home or business they inhabit. As you've learned reading this book, most ghosts and spirits are here for a specific reason: they have a goal. By finding out what their goal is, and, in some cases, helping the ghost achieve that goal, it will put the ghost at peace, as well as bring peace to the building the ghost is haunting. It's a win-win situation.

In my opinion, roughly 75 percent of all alleged paranormal activity can be debunked, and an earthly reason for that activity can be found. It's the other 25 percent that the majority of paranormal researchers spend their lives looking for.

There are many different types of ghosts, spirits, and negative entities that could, at almost any time, decide to invade your home and disrupt the lives of you and your family.

In the majority of cases, a spirit coming into a home is not the occupant's fault, but there are times when we invite ghosts to share our space, although perhaps inadvertently. Ever hear the saying "It's all great fun until someone gets hurt"? It's a similar principle with paranormal activity. In jest, someone might pull out a Ouija board, have a séance, or practice some form of magic that they aren't well schooled in. We've all done it; I know I have.

We either don't believe in the world of the paranormal, or we don't believe anything will ever happen to us.

The bottom line is that the paranormal is not a game; it's not to be played with or used as a night's entertainment. The world of the paranormal is an unpredictable place where bad things can and do happen to unsuspecting people. Unfortunately for most people, by the time they've realized they've made a mistake, it's too late.

But what about the people who don't play with the paranormal as if it were some parlor game, people who are just minding their own business and happen to accidently fall into the web of the paranormal? These people are the real victims, and there are certain types of ghosts, spirits, and demons, among other entities, that are predators and will be like a cat stalking its prey.

Yet there are ghosts and spirits that are friendly and helpful, such as those that just want to stay in touch with loved ones or with the living. They don't mean to scare or frighten us; they just want to be heard or acknowledged in some way. It is we who may perceive all ghosts and spirits to be "bad," when in reality not all of them are. Just as in the world of the living, there is good and bad.

The bottom line is that before you jump to conclusions, get the facts. Pay attention to the behavior of the ghost and determine if anyone in your family is being harmed, and not just startled or scared.

Remember that a calm, assertive attitude is your first line of defense against ghosts and spirits. I can't stress enough how important it is to let them know that you are in control and that you have every intention of claiming your space, be it your home or place of business.

However, if you are feeling overwhelmed, emotionally drained, frustrated, or unsure about how to deal with the paranormal activity occurring in your home, you should seek out a qualified paranormal investigator to assist you in your endeavors. Attempting to get a ghost or spirit to leave your home while you are in an emotionally weakened, frightened, and/or vulnerable position could, in some cases, only make matters worse. It's always better to err on the side of caution when dealing with any type of paranormal activity.

I'm sure most of you have seen all those ghost-hunting shows on television, and, for the most part, they're really very good. Paranormal investigators, like everyone else, are only human. We get scared by some of the paranormal experiences we encounter just as anyone else would. However, with many of us, our curiosity, for the most part, overrides our fear.

When it comes to the topic of demons and other inhumans such as elementals, there are many schools of thought. Many people, including many paranormal investigators, do not believe in demons but believe there are only negative ghosts or spirits. Obviously, these people have never come across a demon or another type of inhuman, or else their opinions would change very fast.

I used to share their line of thought. I didn't believe in demons either, but then I ran headfirst into one and had my mind changed for me. It was, to say the least, a life-changing experience. Since my encounter with the demon, I view nothing the same way as I did before.

Even as I write this, I think back to that time and how completely naïve I was then. I mean, I'd had an experience during my teenage years that should have made me realize that demons do exist, yet I refused to acknowledge that very simple fact even though it was staring me right in the face.

Throughout my life I've been witness to many unexplainable and bizarre paranormal activities that I simply can't find a logical explanation for. There have been times when I just wanted to walk away from the whole paranormal world and have a "normal" life, and I'm sure many other paranormal investigators have felt the same way from time to time. But something always happens to lure us back in, like a fish to water.

The bottom line is this: not everyone is cut out to deal with the paranormal, and that's nothing to be ashamed or embarrassed about. Don't be too afraid or too proud to ask for help if you need it. Skilled paranormal investigators will not think you're crazy, strange, or weird when you tell them about the paranormal events you are experiencing.

I also want to reiterate what I, and many others who can see and communicate with the dead, actually do. Many people believe that the gift of being able to see dead people comes from God, or whatever higher power they believe in. Still others believe that those of us with this ability get our gift from the devil, and that what we do is evil or bad.

Science has shown us that we use only about one-third of our brains. That leaves what the other two-thirds of our brains do open for debate. I believe that people who can do what I do, and have other "psychic" gifts, just use a part of their brain that other people don't.

In other words, I believe that the brains of people who are "gifted" or "psychic" are just wired a little bit differently from those in the people who don't think they have any "gifts."

I also believe that everyone has the ability to be psychic in some way, and for whatever reason most people either choose not to use their gifts or aren't aware that they have them.

It's been my experience that, whether or not they are aware they have them, people who choose to use their gifts act almost like a magnet for the paranormal. Others may think that, because we're aware of our gifts, everything that happens we attribute to a ghost or spirit. That simply isn't the case. Most people who are gifted have also learned to tell the difference between a legitimate paranormal event and an incident that can be logically explained.

To those of you who are living in silent terror because of paranormal events going on in your home or place of business, don't be afraid to tell someone or ask for help.

There's absolutely no reason to live in fear in your home or allow someone in your family to be terrorized by a spirit.

Many people are willing, ready, and able to help you. All you have to do is reach out, and someone will be there.

In closing, I want you to know that my help is only an e-mail away. If you're experiencing seemingly paranormal events for which you can't find a logical explanation, you can always e-mail me, at debichestnut@yahoo.com.

Recommended Reading

Belanger, Michelle. *The Ghost Hunter's Survival Guide: Protection Techniques for Encounters with the Paranormal.* Woodbury, MN: Llewellyn Publications, 2009.

Berger, Ruth. *They Don't See What I See: How to Talk with Loved Ones Who Have Crossed Over.* San Francisco: Weiser Books, 2002.

Charles, Louis. *Helping Ghosts: A Guide to Understanding Lost Spirits from Angels & Ghosts, Volume 1.* Scotts Valley, CA: CreateSpace, 2010.

Chestnut, Debi. *So You Want to Be a Ghost Hunter?* Rockville, MD: Oaklight/Dreamz-Work Productions, 2009.

Crowe, Catherine. *The Night Side of Nature.* New York: J. S. Redfield, 1850.

Davidson, Wilma. *Spirit Rescue: A Simple Guide to Talking with Ghosts and Freeing Earthbound Souls.* Woodbury, MN: Llewellyn Publications, 2006.

Elliott, Charles Wyllys. *Mysteries; or, Glimpses of the Supernatural.* New York: Harper & Brothers, 1852.

Goode, Caron B. *Kids Who See Ghosts: How to Guide Them Through Fear.* San Francisco: Weiser Books, 2010.

Goodwyn, Melba. *Ghost Worlds: A Guide to Poltergeists, Portals, Ecto-Mist & Spirit Behavior.* Woodbury, MN: Llewellyn Publications, 2007.

Persinger, Michael A. *The Paranormal.* New York: MSS Information, 1974.

Snow, Tiffany. *Psychic Gifts in the Christian Life: Tools to Connect.* Issaquah, WA: Spirit Journey Books, 2003.

Webster, Richard. *Psychic Protection for Beginners: Creating a Safe Haven for Home & Family.* Woodbury, MN: Llewellyn Publications, 2010.

To Write to the Author

If you wish to contact the author or would like more information about this book, please write to the author in care of Llewellyn Worldwide and we will forward your request. Both the author and the publisher appreciate hearing from you and learning of your enjoyment of this book and how it has helped you. Llewellyn Worldwide cannot guarantee that every letter written to the author can be answered, but all will be forwarded. Please write to:

Debi Chestnut
℅ Llewellyn Worldwide
2143 Wooddale Drive
Woodbury, MN 55125-2989

Please enclose a self-addressed stamped envelope for reply, or $1.00 to cover costs. If outside the USA, enclose an international postal reply coupon.

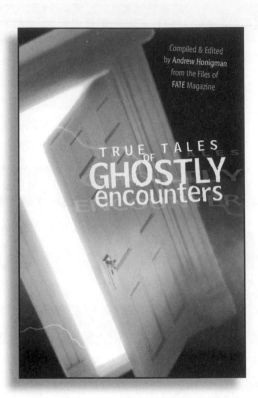

Compiled & Edited
by Andrew Honigman
from the Files of
FATE Magazine

TRUE TALES
OF
GHOSTLY
encounters

True Tales of Ghostly Encounters

COMPILED AND EDITED BY ANDREW HONIGMAN

FATE magazine has published thousands of ghost stories: true experiences of ordinary people who have had extraordinary encounters with the hereafter. Compiled and edited by Andrew Honigman, this collection features the best of these chilling, bizarre, and heartwarming tales. These detailed accounts of messages, gifts, blessings, and assistance from the spirit world provide remarkable proof of life after death.

978-0-7387-0989-5, 312 pp., 5³⁄₁₆ x 8   **$14.95**

Psychic Protection for Beginners
Creating a Safe Haven for Home & Family

RICHARD WEBSTER

Everyone wants a home that is safe and protected. With this friendly and accessible guide to psychic protection and defense, you can ensure the safety and well-being of your home and loved ones.

Bestselling author Richard Webster presents this extensive collection of time-tested and practical methods for psychic protection. Learn to activate the shielding properties of gems and crystals, pendulums, candles, amulets and charms, incense and herbs, the body's chakras (energy centers), and more. Webster's simple yet powerful activities and rituals enable you to block psychic attacks, release negativity, strengthen your aura, and engage in prayer and angel communion to create a safe, nurturing, and harmonious home.

978-0-7387-2060-9, 312 pp., 5³⁄₁₆ x 8   **$15.95**

To order, call 1-877-NEW-WRLD
Prices subject to change without notice
Order at Llewellyn.com 24 hours a day, 7 days a week!

THE
CASE FOR
GHOSTS

AN OBJECTIVE LOOK AT THE PARANORMAL
J. ALLAN DANELEK

The Case for Ghosts
An Objective Look at the Paranormal

J. ALLAN DANELEK

What are ghosts? Can anyone become one? How do they interact with time and space? Stripping away the sensationalism linked to this contentious topic, J. Allan Danelek presents a well-researched study of a phenomenon that has fascinated mankind for centuries.

Analyzing theories that support and debunk these supernatural events, Danelek objectively explores hauntings, the ghost psyche, spirit communication, and spirit guides. He also investigates spirit photography, EVPs, ghost-hunting tools, Ouija boards, and the darker side of the ghost equation—malevolent spirits and demon possession. Whether you're a ghost enthusiast or a skeptic, *The Case for Ghosts* promises amazing insights into the spirit realm.

978-0-7387-0865-2, 240 pp., 6 x 9   **$12.95**

OVER 1000 HAUNTED PLACES YOU CAN EXPERIENCE

THE GHOST HUNTER'S FIELD GUIDE

RICH NEWMAN

The Ghost Hunter's Field Guide

Over 1,000 Haunted Places You Can Experience

RICH NEWMAN

Ghost-hunting isn't just on television. More and more paranormal investigation groups are popping up across the nation. To get in on the action, you need to know where to go.

The Ghost Hunter's Field Guide features over one thousand haunted places around the country in all fifty states. Visit battlefields, theaters, saloons, hotels, museums, resorts, parks, and other sites teeming with ghostly activity. Each location—haunted by the spirits of murderers, Civil War soldiers, plantation slaves, and others—is absolutely safe and accessible.

This indispensable reference guide features over one hundred photos and offers valuable information for each location, including the tales behind the haunting and the kind of paranormal phenomena commonly experienced there: apparitions, shadow shapes, phantom aromas, telekinetic activity, and more.

978-0-7387-2088-3, 432 pp., 6 x 9   **$17.95**

How to Be a Ghost Hunter

RICHARD SOUTHALL

So you want to investigate a haunting? This book is full of practical advice used in the author's own ghost-hunting practice. Find out whether you're dealing with a ghost, spirit, or an entity … and discover the one time when you should stop what you're doing and call in an exorcist. Learn the four-phase procedure for conducting an effective investigation, and how to capture paranormal phenomena on film, record disembodied sounds and voices on tape, assemble an affordable ghost-hunting kit, and form your own paranormal group.

For anyone with time and little money to spend on equipment, this book will help you maintain a healthy sense of skepticism and thoroughness while you search for authentic evidence of the paranormal.

978-0-7387-0312-1, 168 pp., 5³⁄₁₆ x 8   **$12.95**

wayward
spirits
&
earthbound
souls

true tales of ghostly crossings

ANSON V. GOGH

Wayward Spirits & Earthbound Souls

True Tales of Ghostly Crossings

ANSON V. GOGH

Meet the colorful array of lost souls, earthbound spirits, and troubled (or troublemaking) entities that spirit wrangler and psychic clairvoyant Anson V. Gogh has encountered in her years of working with the dead. There's Pool Hall Jenny, a personable and vivacious spirit who doesn't want to leave the neon and the nightlife. Ida Mae, a powerful and magically skilled ghost, is determined to destroy her former daughter-in-law's life. The chivalrous and polite Men in Gray are the spirits of Confederate soldiers awaiting their next orders.

In this fascinating collection of true stories, Gogh shares her most interesting, difficult, and unusual cases. Helping an escaped slave reunite with his family, finding justice for a young girl murdered in 1896, even crossing over a group of souls at Wal-Mart—it's all in a day's work. *Wayward Spirits & Earthbound Souls* also includes advice that readers (whether psychic or not) can use to help lost spirits cross over to the other side.

978-0-7387-1935-1, 216 pp., 6 x 9   **$15.95**

To order, call 1-877-NEW-WRLD
Prices subject to change without notice
Order at Llewellyn.com 24 hours a day, 7 days a week!

TRUE
HAUNTINGS

SPIRITS WITH
A PURPOSE

HAZEL M.
DENNING, PH.D.

True Hauntings
Spirits with a Purpose

HAZEL M. DENNING, PH.D.

How do ghosts feel and think? Do they suffer? Does death automatically promote them to a paradise, or as some believe, a hell? In *True Hauntings*, psychic researcher Dr. Hazel M. Denning recounts the real-life case histories of the earthbound spirits—both benevolent and malevolent—she has investigated. She also explores spirit possession, psychic attack, mediumship, and spirit guides.

978-1-56718-218-7, 240 pp., 6 x 9　　　　　　　**$14.95**